ROGERS MEMORIAL
LIBRARY

D0616038

YANKEE'S
NEW ENGLAND
↠ ADVENTURES ↞

YANKEE'S
NEW ENGLAND
ADVENTURES

OVER 400 ESSENTIAL THINGS TO SEE AND DO

BY THE EDITORS OF *YANKEE* MAGAZINE

Edited by Eric D. Lehman

Globe Pequot

GUILFORD, CONNECTICUT

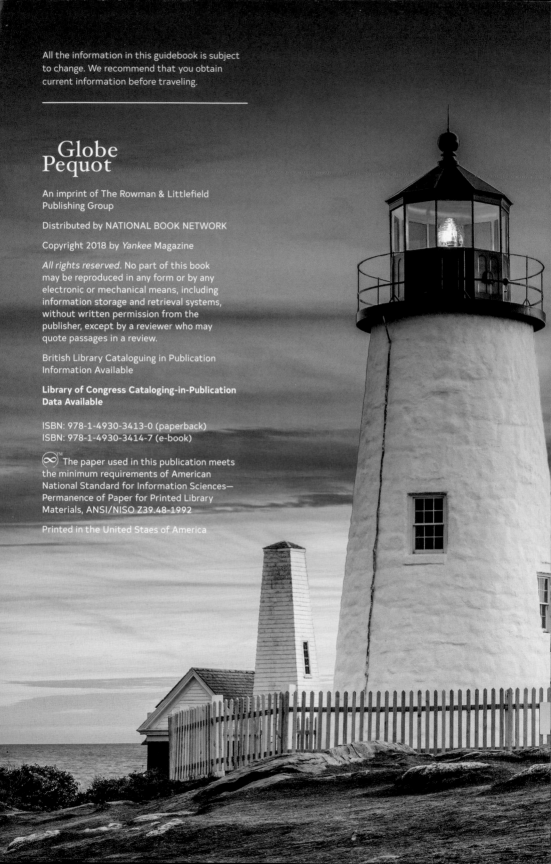

All the information in this guidebook is subject
to change. We recommend that you obtain
current information before traveling.

Globe
Pequot

An imprint of The Rowman & Littlefield
Publishing Group

Distributed by NATIONAL BOOK NETWORK

Copyright 2018 by *Yankee* Magazine

All rights reserved. No part of this book
may be reproduced in any form or by any
electronic or mechanical means, including
information storage and retrieval systems,
without written permission from the
publisher, except by a reviewer who may
quote passages in a review.

British Library Cataloguing in Publication
Information Available

**Library of Congress Cataloging-in-Publication
Data Available**

ISBN: 978-1-4930-3413-0 (paperback)
ISBN: 978-1-4930-3414-7 (e-book)

♾™ The paper used in this publication meets
the minimum requirements of American
National Standard for Information Sciences—
Permanence of Paper for Printed Library
Materials, ANSI/NISO Z39.48-1992

Printed in the United Staes of America

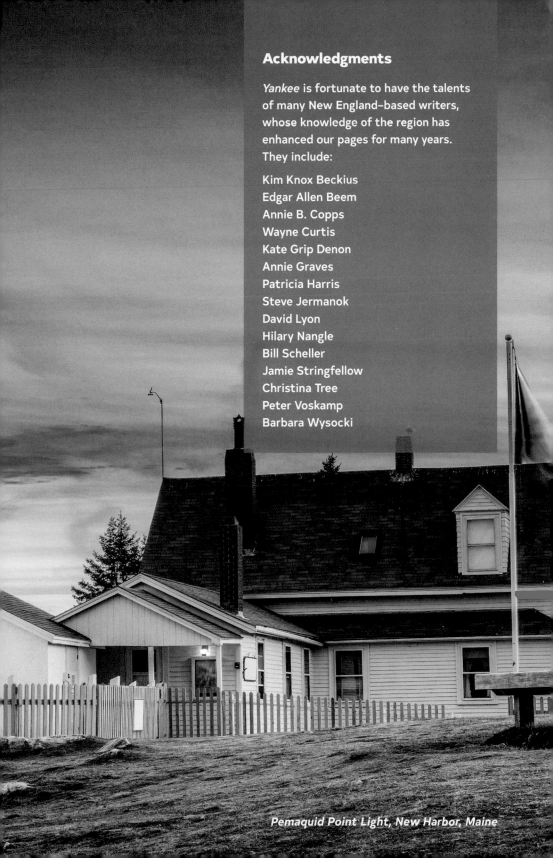

Acknowledgments

Yankee is fortunate to have the talents of many New England–based writers, whose knowledge of the region has enhanced our pages for many years. They include:

Kim Knox Beckius
Edgar Allen Beem
Annie B. Copps
Wayne Curtis
Kate Grip Denon
Annie Graves
Patricia Harris
Steve Jermanok
David Lyon
Hilary Nangle
Bill Scheller
Jamie Stringfellow
Christina Tree
Peter Voskamp
Barbara Wysocki

Pemaquid Point Light, New Harbor, Maine

NEW ENGLAND

CANADA

MAINE

VERMONT

NEW
HAMPSHIRE

Atlantic
Ocean

NEW
YORK

MASSACHUSETTS

CONNECTICUT

RHODE
ISLAND

CONTENTS

Introduction   viii

CONNECTICUT   1

RHODE ISLAND   29

MASSACHUSETTS   63

MAINE   115

NEW HAMPSHIRE   147

VERMONT   179

Photo Credits   218
Index   219

INTRODUCTION

We all have an innate need to explore, to strike out for new destinations or to simply connect more deeply with places we've always known and loved. And no place I know lets you see and experience as much—from sea to mountains to deep clear lakes to storybook villages and world-class museums, all within a few hours of one another—as New England does.

For nearly five decades now, I've lived and worked in New England. There are few nooks and crannies of this compact region that I haven't seen. Yes, it's small: just six states, with one, Rhode Island, being the nation's smallest. You can zip in and out of "Little Rhody" in the time it takes the Red Sox to play one game. The other states—Connecticut, Massachusetts, Vermont, New Hampshire, Maine—can fit inside Nebraska and still leave room to stretch out. But New England is vast enough to contain, for instance, intellectual powerhouses such as Harvard and Yale as well as one-room schools on tiny islands, whose families care just as deeply that their children excel.

New England is gleaming Boston; vibrant Providence, a city reborn with artists and craftspeople; bustling Portland, whose restaurants rival the country's best. New England is also Maine's unorganized territories—those wild lands in the north, inhabited by some 8,000 people, that compose nearly half of the state's area.

New England is Logan International Airport. It's also Greenville, Maine, where floatplanes lift off from Moosehead Lake to deliver fishermen to cabins so remote that the only sounds are wind, coyotes, bobcats, and loons.

New England is Newport, Rhode Island, where magnificent yachts ply Narragansett Bay, but it's also Newport, New Hampshire, home to sugarhouses and apple orchards. New England is miles of warm sand along the shores of Martha's Vineyard and Nantucket. It's also home to Mount Washington, where adventurers have long understood the need to respect what 6,288 feet of altitude means when strong winds come through.

And visitors can see all this in a matter of days—if only they have someone to lead the way.

Yankee's New England Adventures: Over 400 Essential Things to See and Do is our invitation to come explore the corner of America we know and love. *Yankee* has been telling New England's story since 1935, and we're always eager to share it. So we opened our archives to the team at Globe Pequot, whose talented editors and designers worked with us to create the book you hold in your hands.

In its pages you'll find villages to wander, scenic drives that will urge you to stop time and again for photos, lakes so inviting you'll grapple with the decision: swim, kayak, or simply bask onshore? And of course you'll find the iconic coastal towns where lobster boats chug in and out of the harbors, where seafood shacks perch on wharves and the scent of freshly cooked seafood hangs everywhere.

It's all in here. May you enjoy your adventures as much as we've enjoyed putting this together.

Mel Allen

Mel Allen
Editor, *Yankee*

CONNECTICUT

THE NUTMEG STATE

As the "gateway to New England," Connecticut is many a visitor's first look at this storied land of white-steepled churches, brilliant town greens, and sparkling-blue Atlantic waters (not to mention sophisticated cities, great food, and some seriously competitive outlet shopping).

The state that gave the world Frisbees and submarines, the artificial heart and Pez candy, is a land of contrasts—and it's so compact, you can fill each vacation day with an array of adventures. Dive into the past at historic villages nestled into rolling hills that were first settled in the 1600s, or stroll waterfronts that once thronged with the tall ships of the whaling era. Arts and culture, too, have made their mark on this state: the American Impressionism movement put down early roots here, while the stars of Broadway have long brought their talents to Connecticut playhouses.

From the expanse of beaches that unfurls along Long Island Sound to the country landscapes of the Litchfield Hills and the Last Green Valley, there are endless opportunities to escape into nature. But given the lively mix of vineyards and restaurants, museums and performance halls, antiques emporiums and shopping outlets, there are just as many reasons to join the crowd. In sum, Connecticut is beauty, brains (don't forget Yale University), and entertainment, all in one dynamic package.

CONNECTICUT ESSENTIALS

WESTERN HILLS AND GOLD COAST

BANTAM CINEMA, BANTAM

The first moviegoers to escape reality inside Bantam's barnlike, two-screen theater watched silent flicks with organ accompaniment. That was 1927, and Connecticut's oldest continuously operating movie house finally ditched its 1930s-vintage equipment for a digital projection system in 2013. But, if they ever abandon real butter, those who adore both the popcorn and eclectic films will surely revolt. *860-567-1916; bantamcinema.com*

CANTON BARN, CANTON

Forget eBay and experience the old-fashioned excitement at an auction in a classic New England barn built c. 1820. Most Saturday nights, auctioneer Richard Wacht and his partner, Susan Goralski, disperse entire estates before your eyes, and there's no buyer's premium and no reserve. Order a slice of homemade pie, grab a seat cushion, and raise your hand to bid. From fine furnishings to quirky possessions, everything's going home with new owners. *860-693-0601; cantonbarn.com*

FARMINGTON RIVER TUBING, NEW HARTFORD

Only 20 miles from the house where Mark Twain penned his classic *Huckleberry Finn*, you'll find a chance to emulate his timeless hero, by floating down the Farmington River on a bright-yellow inner tube. Your 2½-mile stretch of the 81-mile-long river begins at Satan's Kingdom Gorge. You'll encounter 3 sets of frothy rapids along the way, but there will be plenty of time spent floating through peaceful drifts of flat water on a stretch of the Farmington so pristine it has earned federal "wild and scenic" status. *860-693-6465; farmingtonrivertubing.com*

GLEBE HOUSE MUSEUM & GERTRUDE JEKYLL GARDEN, WOODBURY

Famed horticulturist Gertrude Jekyll designed more than 400 gardens in Europe, but lent her touch to only 3 in the U.S. Connecticut's Glebe House Museum boasts the sole survivor. Along with the lovely garden itself, visitors are always enthralled by the story of how Jekyll's plans for the Glebe House grounds were lost, then rediscovered after a half-century and brought to life. *203-263-2855; theglebehouse.org*

THE GLASS HOUSE, NEW CANAAN

"I have very expensive wallpaper," architect Philip Johnson once joked about his iconic Glass House, built in 1949 on his 47-acre property in New Canaan, Connecticut. The single-story, 1,815-square-foot structure makes a dramatic architectural statement thanks to its floor-to-ceiling glass exterior and open floor plan. Now owned by the National Trust for Historic Preservation, the property is dotted with a dozen other modernist structures designed by Johnson, many of which are included on the various tour options. *866-811-4111; theglasshouse.org*

HILL-STEAD MUSEUM, FARMINGTON

One of America's first women architects and the daughter of Cleveland iron magnate Alfred Pope, Theodate Pope Riddle designed this distinguished Colonial Revival home as a country estate for her globetrotting parents. At the turn of the last century, the Popes toured Europe

The Farmington River

Gertrude Jekyll Garden (Glebe House, Seabury Society)

annually, often purchasing blurry Impressionist art straight from starving artists like Degas, Monet, Manet, and Cassatt, before they became famous. Mounted

DID YOU KNOW? The Connecticut Freedom Trail leads you to over 130 sites that celebrate the accomplishments of the state's African-American community. *ctfreedomtrail.org*

within reach over fireplaces and on walls, the paintings are as accessible to visitors as they were to the home's original residents. *860-677-4787; hillstead.org*

EXPLORE LITCHFIELD HILLS

The Connecticut you dream about becomes reality in the Litchfield Hills, the area roughly bounded by Route 8 to the east, Massachusetts's Berkshire County to the north, and New York State to the west. Travel the hill towns in autumn and you'll see those dream images in living color. From Route 8 you can drive up the hill to the Litchfield town green with its Greek Revival Congregational Church and the stately mansions of North and South streets, and head west toward forest-and-farm-ringed Lake Waramaug straddling New Preston, Kent, and Warren. You can continue west to the state's most heart-stoppingly beautiful cascade at Kent Falls, then north to the covered bridge over the Housatonic in West Cornwall, an architectural marvel in 1864 and a photographer's favorite subject today. In the far northwest corner of the state you can climb Bear Mountain in Salisbury, 2,316 feet high, the state's tallest peak and an incomparable outlook yielding panoramic vistas.

THE MARITIME AQUARIUM, NORWALK

Housed in a renovated 19th-century ironworks, this aquarium ranks as one of Connecticut's top tourist attractions, and it's easy to see why. Visitors have a chance to get an up-close look at more than 1,000 animals representing the wildlife of Long Island Sound and beyond, most dramatically in the 110,000-gallon Open Ocean tank: Take a seat in the darkened viewing area and enjoy the aquatic ballet, as sand tiger sharks, roughtail stingrays, stripers, and bluefish circumnavigate the tank while music plays quietly in the background. Elsewhere you'll find river otters, green sea turtles, and harbor seals, plus touch tanks and an Ocean Playspace for wee ones, and the largest IMAX movie

The namesake of Weir Farm National Historic Site 19th-Century American Impressionist J. Alden We

theater in Connecticut. The aquarium anchors a revitalized waterfront district, known as SoNo, that's packed with cosmopolitan restaurants and trendy galleries—so whether or not you have your own spawn in tow, you've got the makings of a perfect day-trip. *203-852-0700; maritime aquarium.org*

SHEFFIELD ISLAND, SOUTH NORWALK

Though retired as guardian for ships at sea since 1920, the Sheffield Island Lighthouse today serves as a beacon for tourists, who can see its light glittering from the Norwalk coast. The c. 1868 stone lighthouse with its 44-foot tower is the main attraction on the westernmost of the Norwalk Islands chain, but the 30-minute ferry out to the island is also a treat, and onshore there are nature trails to explore. On clear days, you can see New York's skyline from the top of the lighthouse and on Thursdays nights in the summer, the Norwalk Seaport Association hosts festive

> **TRAVEL TIP:** From 1892 until 1958 the island of Pleasure Beach off of Bridgeport and Stratford was home to a popular amusement park, and today you can take a ferry from downtown Bridgeport and visit this quiet, lonely beach. *bridgeportct.gov/pleasurebeach*

clambakes in a pavilion next to the lighthouse. *203-838-9444; seaport.org*

TOPSMEAD STATE FOREST, LITCHFIELD

Edith Morton Chase left her beloved summer retreat to the state in 1972 with the stipulation that it "be kept in a state of natural beauty." Today, her fairy-tale English Tudor cottage atop a picturesque hill is a jewel of the state park system. So why do visitors often have this place to themselves? Perhaps it's the absence of signs pointing the way. That's just as well, for when you do find your way to "top of the meadow," you will feel as if fortune has smiled upon you. Stroll the paths that meander through woods and hayfields or picnic on the sweeping lawn in view of the mansion's formal gardens. *860-567-5694; ct.gov/deep*

WEIR FARM NATIONAL HISTORIC SITE, BRANCHVILLE

Bring a sketch pad to the former summer country retreat of Impressionist painter J. Alden Weir, because the rustic landscape of Weir's home, studio, barns, and outbuildings is sure to get your creative energies flowing. An inspiration to Weir and other artists for over a century, the 200-year-old farm is now the only National Park Service site dedicated to American painting. Rangers offer tours of the historic Weir House and welcome visitors to explore the property's 60 acres of forest and farmland. *203-834-1896; nps.gov/wefa*

WESTPORT COUNTRY PLAYHOUSE, WESTPORT

It's not fair to call the Westport Country Playhouse a summer stock theater, since its performances begin in April and run into November. However, it comes most alive on those balmy summer evenings when the nearly 90-year-old theater puts on productions in a simple red barn whose first life was as a tannery in 1835. Over the decades it has drawn performers known around the world, like Liza Minnelli, Paul Newman, Joanne Woodward, Henry Fonda, Jessica Tandy, Olivia de Havilland, and Gene Wilder. Today the nonprofit theater remains a cornerstone of a small town's cultural past and present, a reminder that country life and great theater can co-exist, at least on the wealthy Gold Coast of Connecticut. *888-927-7529; westportplayhouse.org*

CONNECTICUT RIVER VALLEY

BUSHNELL PARK CAROUSEL, HARTFORD

Hartford's treasured merry-go-round is over a century old and one of fewer than 200 survivors of carousels' golden age. Visitors can ride 48 meticulously restored, hand-carved wooden horses in a pavilion renovated with heat and indoor restrooms to enable year-round operation. Spins on this work of art remain a remarkably low $1. *860-585-5411; thecarouselmuseum.org*

Bushnell Park Carousel Horse

FARMINGTON RIVER TRAIL, FARMINGTON

Just a 10-minute drive from the hubbub of Hartford, cyclists can bike into some of the prettiest landscapes in Connecticut on this 18-mile recreational trail between Farmington and Simsbury. Built on the former Central New England Railroad bed, the largely paved trail runs along a stretch of the Farmington River and provides plentiful opportunities for stops and side trips, like the beautiful old industrial village of Collinsville. Cyclists who want to keep going can connect to the Farmington Canal Heritage Trail, which when complete will sprawl all the way from the Berkshire foothills to Long Island Sound. *860-202-3928; fchtrail.org*

DID YOU KNOW? The Reverend Sylvester Graham of West Suffield was a 19th-century reformer who advocated temperance: a vegetarian diet of plain, unseasoned, high-fiber food, and home baking using his own signature coarse grind of whole-wheat flour, which threw out the germ but retained the bran. The graham cracker, well known by the 1880s, is still one of America's favorite cookies.

Gillette Castle

DINOSAUR STATE PARK, ROCKY HILL

In 1966, a worker excavating this location for a new state building saw something unusual—a dinosaur track. Turns out that 200 million years ago this was the stomping ground of dilophosaurus, an 8-foot-tall, 20-foot-long dinosaur. Today this 63-acre park encompasses the largest dinosaur-track site in North America. Indoors under a giant geodesic dome, you can see a dramatic display of 500 tracks with dioramas and exhibits, while outdoors, kids whose parents call ahead and bring their own materials can make plaster casts of tracks. Afterwards, the whole family can picnic on the grounds, explore 2 miles of trails, and walk a timeline that brings home just what Johnny-come-latelys we humans are. *860-529-5816; dinosaurstatepark.org*

EAGLES OF THE CONNECTICUT RIVER

From January through March, the picturesque towns of the lower Connecticut River play host to more than 100 wintering bald eagles, the largest concentration in New England. Bare branches make it easy to see these majestic birds when they gather along the water, looking for open areas to feed from when many northern waters are frozen solid. The Audubon Society out of Haddam and the Connecticut River Museum in Essex offer naturalist-led eagle-watch tours on heated boats along the river. Don't forget to make reservations. *ctaudubon.org; ctrivermuseum.org*

GILLETTE CASTLE, EAST HADDAM

William Gillette made a fortune playing Sherlock Holmes onstage at the turn of the last century, but judging from the medieval-style fortress he designed on a vista overlooking the Connecticut River, he might have been better suited to play King Arthur. Now the centerpiece of a namesake state park, this hilltop castle is a monument to Gillette's inventiveness

Goodspeed Opera House

and eccentricity, with 47 different door locks, a great room, and a balcony for dramatic entrances. Visitors can tour the 24-room behemoth, walk the grounds over trestles and through tunnels, and enjoy scene-stealing views across the river. *860-526-2336; ct.gov/deep*

GOODSPEED OPERA HOUSE, EAST HADDAM

At this 6-story, Victorian "wedding cake" theater on the Connecticut River, you can still feel the thrill of the musicals birthed here since 1876, including *Annie,*

Essex Steam Train

Shenandoah, and *Man of La Mancha*, and perhaps catch another one destined for greatness. The play's the thing, though there's also drama in the river views from the lounge and vintage charm in the Green Room. *860-873-8668. goodspeed.org*

ESSEX STEAM TRAIN & RIVERBOAT, ESSEX

By the mid-1800s the lower Connecticut River was lined with more than 50 shipyards, and its waters saw boats returning from international waters with spices from the West Indies and ivory tusks from Zanzibar. One result of that newly acquired wealth was the collection of Colonial and Federal-style mansions that still border the water's edge on the outskirts of Essex. On a 2½-hour steam train and riverboat tour of the Connecticut River Valley, you'll pass these classic estates, including the Goodspeed Opera House and Gillette Castle. Look for special rides like the Swallow Sunset during the autumn migrations or the North Pole Express during the holidays. *800-377-3987; essexsteamtrain.com*

HAMMONASSET BEACH STATE PARK, MADISON

From 1919 to 1925, the state anted up $185,000 for 565 shorefront acres, and today its premier waterfront park covers more than 900. This 2-mile golden crescent is hands down the best public beach in Connecticut, spring, summer, and fall. It's perfect for swimming, boating, and fishing, while the acreage is ideal for playing ball, picnicking, and camping. The state—and all of us—got one great deal. *203-245-2785; ct.gov/deep*

DID YOU KNOW? Where the Salmon and Moodus Rivers meet in East Haddam is the center of mysterious minor earth tremors known by Native Americans and terrified colonial settlers as the Moodus Noises. Today, these low rumblings deep underground provide "local color" rather than nightmares.

GRISWOLD INN, ESSEX

Having survived a British attack on Essex during the War of 1812, this inn and tavern has been operating continuously from 1776 to this day, making it the oldest such institution in the nation. And you'll sense this the moment you enter the dining rooms and central Tap Room, which are burnished with so much history it's difficult to simply sit down and eat. Over here are steamboat prints by Currier & Ives, over there, an original Norman Rockwell sketch, and in a wall-mounted case, a collection of firearms dating as far back as the 15th century. The main dining room is constructed from a dismantled New Hampshire covered bridge and the unique, barrel-ceilinged Tap Room was a 1735 schoolhouse. The food is classic pub fare that's as solid as the building's foundation: tasty burgers; thick, creamy chowder; and crispy fish and chips. *860-767-1776; griswoldinn.com*

LONG WHARF THEATRE, NEW HAVEN

The Long Wharf is a Tony Award–winning theater in the unlikeliest of places, amid a string of meatpacking plants and food factories, jammed between two highways. Nevertheless, Al Pacino, Mia Farrow, Christopher Walken, and Nathan Lane are among the luminaries who have graced its stage. The dubious locale is eclipsed by the theater's 40-year reputation of presenting classic dramas and cutting-edge new works, many of which are tested on New Haven's sophisticated audiences before taking a shot at Broadway. *203-787-4282; longwharf.org*

LOUIS' LUNCH, NEW HAVEN

When you stop into this fabled birthplace of the hamburger tell 'em to "burn one, take it through the garden, and pin a rose on it," which translates to grilled, with lettuce, tomato, and onion. Grab a "stretch" (Coke) or a "blonde with sand" (coffee with cream and sugar), and whatever you do, don't ask for ketchup. Few eateries can survive with just 25 seats and a handful of menu items, but this one, on the National Register of Historic Places, has been going strong since 1895. A trip to New Haven isn't complete without a Louis' burger. *203-562-5507; louislunch.com*

→ NEW HAVEN PIZZA WARS

Who makes the better pizza, **Frank Pepe Pizzeria Napoletana** (*203-865-5762, pepespizzeria.com*) or **Sally's Apizza** (*203-624-5271, sallysapizza.net*)? People have been fighting about it for years, but the folks at these famed New Haven pizzerias—located just a few blocks apart on Wooster Street—pay little heed to the fact that their mutual specialty is the subject of this state's well-publicized "pizza wars." Pepe's opened first, in 1925; Sally's, founded by Pepe's nephew Salvatore Consiglio, opened in 1938. And what they both care about is their pizzas; the feud itself is wholly among the folks who join the perpetual queue outside both eateries, whatever the weather.

The two restaurants have a lot in common. Both make thin-crust "New Haven–style" pies, an American translation of the traditional pizza of Naples, Italy. Both venues cook their pies at blisteringly hot temperatures in coal-fired brick ovens. And both secretly add a touch of some mystical substance that keeps us hankering for more.

At Pepe's, the white clam pie is what elicits our Pavlovian responses. The crispy-yet-chewy crust holds sweet and briny clams, gobs of minced garlic, oregano, a shake of Parmesan, and a healthy drizzle of olive oil.

Yet we're slightly more partial to Sally's for its thin, charred-at-the edges crust; its generous toppings; and its zippy red sauce. It's worth noting that Sally's has recently been sold, after having been owned by the Consiglio family for more than 80 years, but all indications are that the new crew is staying the course.

For pizza lovers who need to sample even more, other joints throughout the county offer similar joys, including New Haven's **Modern Apizza** (*203-776-5306; modernapizza.com*) and West Haven's **Zuppardi's** (*203-934-1949; zuppardisapizza.com*).

Crooner Frank Sinatra used to order his pizza from New Haven and have it brought to New York City. Find out why, and choose a side in the pizza wars.

MARK TWAIN HOUSE & MUSEUM, HARTFORD

Samuel Clemens, aka Mark Twain, spent his best years in this one-of-a-kind Victorian home. It was here that he wrote *Tom Sawyer*, *Huckleberry Finn*, and *A Connecticut Yankee in King Arthur's Court*. Though we generally ascribe qualities of modesty and frugality to New England's old houses, this magnificent mansion speaks of Hartford's heyday as a commercial powerhouse, and its exuberance expresses its owner's larger-than-life personality. The 25-room house is filled with memorabilia, mahogany furniture, and Tiffany decorations. Don't miss the library and the

billiard room, where Twain composed his tales. *860-247-0998; marktwainhouse.org*

OLD WETHERSFIELD

History lovers, architecture fans, and those who simply appreciate the feel of a classic New England village will enjoy strolling through the centuries in Old Wetherfield, the state's oldest and largest historic district. Here, more than 150 homes here predate the Civil War and, often, the Revolutionary War, including the Webb House, in which George Washington met the Comte de Rochambeau to plan their victory, and the Buttolph-Willams House, which inspired the setting for the Newbery Medal–winning book *The Witch of Blackbird Pond*. Walking along these quiet streets, with brick-paver sidewalks shaded by mature trees, you'd never know you were just a stone's throw from busy I-91. *860-721-2800; wethersfieldct.com*

THE PLACE, GUILFORD

The roasted littlenecks arrive at your table in a bath of buttery cocktail sauce, still on a grill grate, straight off the wood fire. Instantly you understand why folks have been pulling off Route 1 since 1971 to savor clams, lobster, bluefish and more. The Place has kept everything the same for four decades, including tree stumps for seats, and a cook-out atmosphere that keeps everyone coming back time and time again. *203-453-9276; theplace guilford.com*

(Left and below) Old Wethersfield's Buttolph-Willams House

SLEEPING GIANT STATE PARK, HAMDEN

Driving up I-91 from New Haven, you can see this mountain ahead of you, resembling an enormous sleeping person under a green sheet of trees. This large state park may be the best place to hike in Connecticut, with an extensive network of trails at various levels of difficulty. If you're looking for a gentle walk to the top of the mountain, the easy-graded Tower Trail is the most popular walking path in the entire state, but that has drawbacks if you want to find peace and quiet. For a challenge, hike from the parking lot down to the river, and then take the blue trail along the edge of the quarry up the "head" of the Giant. This precarious, steep trail has an amazing reward: the spectacular view from the "chin" cliff of New Haven and across the Sound to Long Island. *203-287-5658; sgpa.org*

DID YOU KNOW? The father of America's highways is New Haven's Eli Whitney Blake, who invented the stone crusher in 1851.

THIMBLE ISLAND CRUISES, STONY CREEK

There's an eclectic history to the Thimble Islands, a windswept archipelago that's home to an exclusive summer colony where an invite is required to step ashore. If none is forthcoming, don't worry, you can hop aboard the *Volsunga IV*. As captain Bob Milne pilots the boat past dozens of granite upheavals with names such as Money, Potato, and Mother-in-Law, he delivers a well-rehearsed spiel seasoned with legends about Tom Thumb and Captain Kidd. Touristy? Maybe. But we love it for what it is. *203-481-3345; thimbleislands.com*

(Left and above) The Place

→ ANTIQUING IN CONNECTICUT

Brimming with shops that run the gamut from cluttered bargain basements to rarefied emporiums that could pass for museums, Connecticut has rightly earned its reputation as one of the nation's great antiquing destinations. In the towns most densely packed with yesteryear wares, antiques hunters will find their heads spinning, as practically every house has a sign beckoning you inside. A designated driver and a mapped-out itinerary may come in handy, although more spontaneous treasure hunters may simply choose to stop and shop.

A good place to start is **Woodbury**, nicknamed "the antiques capital of Connecticut." It features 35-plus antiques shops, many situated in the historic residences that line picturesque Main Street, including G. Sergeant (for European formal furniture) and Winsor Antiques (for English/French country furniture). For Swedish accessories and furniture Eleish Van Breems Antiques is just over the border in **Bridgewater**.

You'll find about two dozen small shops between **Litchfield** and **New Preston**, most on "antiques highway" Route 202. This browser-friendly mix of antiques and other shops of collectibles includes Litchfield's Jeffrey Tillou Antiques (for American 18th- and 19th-century furniture, paintings, and folk art), and New Preston's Dawn Hill Antiques (for 18th- and 19th-century Swedish antiques).

At the far southeast end of the state, about 20 shops spread between **Stonington** and **Mystic**. In small, walkable Stonington Borough, antiques shops are the stars of the show; in bigger, bustling Mystic, they are bit players. Try Stonington's Grand and Water for an eclectic mix of vintage décor or Old Mystic's Holly Hock Farm Antiques for furniture by the likes of Fineberg and Margolis.

In the state's northeast corner is the old mill town of **Putnam**, with more than a dozen group shops in a 4-block area, including 4-story The Antiques Marketplace. In the southwest corner, **Stamford** also features multidealer consortiums in converted warehouses on and around Canal Street. Standouts include Avery & Dash, with 23,000 square feet of fine furnishings from the 18th through 20th century, and the Antique and Artisan Gallery, with 150 dealers offering eclectic mix of furniture, décor, and collectibles.

Whether you're looking for a big find to re-sell or just a new decorative lamp, Connecticut's antiques trail offers an entire world to explore. *888-288-4748; ctvisit.com/antiquestrail*

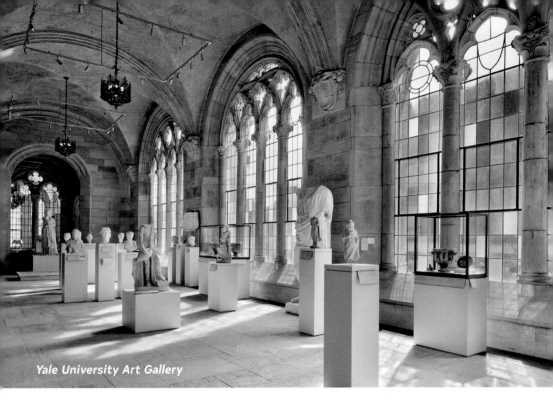
Yale University Art Gallery

WADSWORTH ATHENEUM MUSEUM OF ART, HARTFORD

America's oldest continuously operating public art museum has been growing its collection since the brushstrokes on Hudson River School landscapes were barely dry. A $33 million renovation completed in 2015 has expanded and revitalized exhibit spaces for holdings that now exceed 50,000 works spanning 5,000 years of human creativity. Be sure to visit the Early American furniture and Impressionist collections, and stop for a bite at the artful Museum Café, where menu specials are inspired by current exhibitions. *860-278-2670; thewadsworth.org*

TRAVEL TIP: For a great view of Connecticut's Capital year-round, you can go to the top floor of the Travelers Insurance Company tower (1 Tower Square) in Hartford; take the elevator and then 70 stairs to the top.

YALE UNIVERSITY MUSEUMS, NEW HAVEN

Originally 3 historic buildings now laced together by a recent renovation, the Yale University Art Gallery showcases classic canvases by Hals, Trumbull, and van Gogh, among others. World-class art, all for free. Across the street, and also free to enjoy, is the Yale Center for British Art, the premier collection of British art outside the United Kingdom. Rounding out the cultural three-fer is the Peabody Museum of Natural History, located to the north on Science Hill. Its cache of over 1.2 million objects includes the skeleton of the largest turtle species ever known, 11-feet long from snout to tail. You'll need to pay a small admission fee to see the natural wonders here, but it's worth it. *yale.edu*

Connecticut Shoreline

MYSTIC COUNTRY AND THE EAST

ABBOTT'S LOBSTER IN THE ROUGH, NOANK

In Noank's fishing community full of back-yard gardens and harbor views at every turn, Abbott's is a bona fide institution. Founded in 1947, it has just about anything a shellfish lover could desire but it's best known for a steamed lobster or Connecticut-style hot lobster roll. Abbott's offers a quarter pound of warm, succulent lobster drizzled with butter and served on a toasted hamburger bun; however, those with heartier appetites are welcome to upsize to the 7-oz. "OMG" version or the full-pound "LOL." *860-536-7719; abbottslobster.com*

BLUFF POINT STATE PARK, GROTON

Hikers, bicyclists, and other outdoor types come to this rugged peninsula to savor the pristine coast. The 806-acre

DID YOU KNOW? Despite not being a native species, the sperm whale earned the title of Connecticut's state animal because of its role in the local 19th-century whaling industry.

hiking and birding oasis was a farm for two centuries, and now boasts some of the state's last undisturbed shoreline. Old cart roads meander through woods and meadows to the lofty bluff, where the view of Long Island Sound is stunning. Leave time to hunt for shells on the mile-long barrier beach. Spy on egrets, herons, and other shorebirds in the adjoining salt marsh. *860-444-7591; ct.gov/deep*

THE BOOK BARN, NIANTIC

Want proof that people still have a soft spot for the printed word? Head to Niantic, the coastal village at the nucleus of New England's book trade, where the business that Randi and Maureen White

→ NEW ENGLAND CIDER MILLS

Cider is autumn in liquid form. Whether you prefer the modern innocent version or traditional cider that packs a kick, New England's best cider mills offer a behind-the-scenes look at how apples become drinkable.

Start in Old Mystic, Connecticut at **B.F. Clyde's Cider Mill** (*860-536-3354; bfclydescidermill.com*), which started producing hard cider 135 years ago, and still uses the machinery bought by B.F. Clyde in 1898. Gears clatter, belts rumble and hum, and cider gushes each week during the harvest, as nearly 75 tons of handpicked Hudson Valley apples are transformed into nonalcoholic sweet cider, apple wines, and potent ciders.

Moving north to Ashfield, Massachusetts, you should visit **Bear Swamp Orchard & Cidery** (*413-625-2849; bearswamporchard.com*), with a view of Mount Monadnock and a 7-acre orchard. While you can pick apples or purchase unpasteurized cider, it's the collection of organic hard ciders, made by only a handful of cideries nationwide, that's putting Bear Swamp on the map. Look for

the Prohibition-era New England Style, barrel-aged with brown sugar and raisins.

In Waterbury, Vermont, you'll find **Cold Hollow Cider Mill** (*800-327-7537; coldhollow.com*), with fresh cider coaxed from McIntosh apples grown on Lake Champlain's shores. You can watch it made with a vintage press daily in the fall and twice weekly during quieter seasons. It doesn't all wind up in jugs, though, and you can enjoy cider vinaigrette, cider-chipotle BBQ sauce, and intensely flavored cider jelly. And don't miss the cider doughnuts.

At the fourth-generation family enterprise of **Jaswell's Farm** (*401-231-9043; jaswellsfarm.com*) in Smithfield, Rhode Island, you can peer through observation windows as hundreds of pounds of apples are inspected, brusher-washed, and elevatored up into the chopper. An old-fashioned rack and cloth press applies 2,000 pounds of pressure to the apple pomace, extracting crisp, refreshing cider that's doubly apple-licious when paired with the farm's hand-crafted, 2-pound candy apples.

Bartlett, New Hampshire's **White Mountain Cider Company** (*603-383-9061; ciderconh.com*) makes fresh hot cider doughnuts in the morning. For lunch, stop in for tart, icy cider slushies and deli sandwiches, plus the chance to watch cider-making in progress on fall weekends. In the evening, you can savor cider's grown-up side at the fine-dining restaurant, which exploits the golden liquid's sweet and savory nuances in everything from cider-braised pork to "cidertini" cocktails.

Niantic Book Barn

founded in 1988 with three bookshelves and a yard sale couch has exploded to four locations packed with over 500,000 used books, one of the largest collections in America. The Main Barn complex, with its cats and free coffee, gardens and picnic tables, is the best place to start, and to linger. *860-739-5715; bookbarnniantic.com*

FLORENCE GRISWOLD MUSEUM, OLD LYME

Florence Griswold's boardinghouse became the epicenter of American Impressionism when she hosted preeminent painters like Henry Ward Ranger, Childe Hassam, and Willard Metcalf. Throughout the early 20th century these artistic houseguests painted not only *en plein air* but also on the walls and doors of her dining room. Her house now anchors an 11-acre museum complex that still remains a center of creativity, with a packed calendar of exhibits and programs. *860-434-5542; florencegriswoldmuseum.org*

LAST GREEN VALLEY

With Worcester to the north, Hartford to the west, and Providence to the east, this unspoiled 1,000-square-mile chunk of green and its 35 rural villages are so precious, they've been federally recognized since 1994, when Congress conferred its mouthful of a designation: the Quinebaug and

Shetucket Rivers Valley National Heritage Corridor. More than 70 percent of the Last Green Valley remains field, farmland, and forest, which means a superabundance of hiking, biking, and birding for you. The bulk of the region lies in Connecticut, and,

Florence Griswold Museum

conveniently, the state's second-longest National Scenic Byway, Route 169, glides smack through the middle. Thirty-two charmed, dotted-green miles running north to south, from Woodstock to Lisbon: a collection of lovely little towns strung together like New England pearls, and not a mall in sight. *860-774-3300; thelastgreenvalley.org*

MASHANTUCKET PEQUOT MUSEUM, LEDYARD

Count on the tribal nation that brought you Foxwoods Resort, one of the world's largest casinos, to do preservation and education on an equally grand scale. Opened in 1998, its $135 million state-of-the-art museum and research center spans some 20,000 years of Mashantucket Pequot history. The exhibits, stunning dioramas, and re-created Pequot village will enhance both your awareness

of the natural world and appreciation for this remarkable nation's story. Don't miss the 50-foot-long diorama depicting a caribou hunt 11,000 years ago. *800-411-9671; pequotmuseum.org*

NEW LONDON POST OFFICE

Upon entering the New London post office, you might feel that it's an odd endeavor to peer at art while other folks are standing in line to send off packages. Bring in a letter if you have to, but don't let that distract you from exploring this cavernous edifice, almost a block long in the heart of downtown. And then look up. Below the crown molding are 6 panels of a mural featuring fishermen on a whaling vessel (perfectly suited to recognize New London's maritime history). It was completed at the height of the Great Depression by Thomas La Farge, grandson

Mashantucket Pequot Museum

of the creator of exquisite stained-glass windows in Boston's Trinity Church. La Farge won a competition with the theme of whaling. La Farge commanded a Coast Guard cutter during World War II, and in 1942 it went down off the coast of Newfoundland. The 38-year-old La Farge perished, leaving these murals as his legacy.

STORRS CENTER, STORRS

Connecticut is rightfully proud of UConn's academic and athletic accomplishments, and the new dining and shopping district that's sprung up steps from campus is the place to embrace Huskymania. Tour the university's colorful, Ballard Institute & Museum of Puppetry or the William Benton Museum of Art for free. Shop for UConn gear at the Co-op or dine at Geno Auriemma's namesake grille, and take home the Hall of Fame women's basketball coach's almost-as-famous pasta sauces. *storrscenter.com*

THAMES RIVER HERITAGE PARK, GROTON AND NEW LONDON

It's been envisioned since the 1960s. It was legislated into existence in 1987. And in 2016, Connecticut's first state park without boundaries became a reality. The key to linking Fort Trumbull, Fort Griswold, and more than a dozen smaller historic attractions along the Thames River was a water taxi service, which runs Memorial Day weekend through mid-September. Friday through Sunday you can park your car, board a restored Navy vessel, and plot your sightseeing adventure with a stop for lunch or dinner on New London's historic waterfront. *thamesriverheritagepark.org*

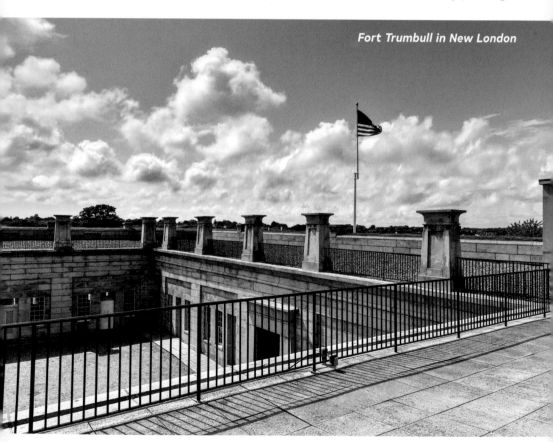

Fort Trumbull in New London

➡️ FLY-FISHING

Fly-fishing, particularly in New England, is not an activity that lends itself to over-planned days. It is more fickle than New England weather because it depends on the weather and the water. And the unpredictable habits of trout and salmon. And the vagaries of hatching insects. Ideal fly-fishing is based on luck, educated guessing, and being out there—day after day, evening after evening.

But fly fishermen are nothing if not gamblers. We take calculated risks and hedge our bets. And for our money, New England boasts some of the best places to cast a line. Connecticut's **Housatonic River** (*ctvisit.com*) flows through the Litchfield Hills to Long Island Sound from the Massachusetts border, and is a top spot in the eastern United States for trout fly-fishing. Specifically, you will find plenty of catch-and-release brown and rainbow trout in two management areas, as well as wild trout on and near the adjacent streams, like Kent Falls.

The **Ammonoosuc River** (*fishnh.com*) in the White Mountains of north-western New Hampshire stretches for 55 miles from the slopes of Mount Washington to the Connecticut River. The Ammonoosuc is especially known for its brook trout, with larger populations in the colder, faster sections of river farther north. The lower section is stocked by the state with brook, brown, and rainbow trout.

If you prefer fly-fishing on flat water, try the **Rangeley Lakes** (*rangeley-maine.com*). Forming the headwaters of the Androscoggin River, the Rangeley chain of lakes is considered one of the best areas in the state to fish for landlocked salmon and brook trout. The latter are native to the area; the salmon were introduced later, and continue to thrive.

Fly-Fishing on the Housatonic

SPOTLIGHT ON
MYSTIC

Of all the New England seaports singing the glory of our nation's maritime heritage, Mystic's voice may be the loudest in the choir (*860-572-9578; mysticchamber .org*). At the heart of this pretty, bustling village, you'll discover the largest maritime museum in the U.S., one of the country's leading aquariums, sightseeing cruises on tall schooners, and restaurants with fresh, abundant seafood.

With 144 buildings and a fleet of wooden ships anchored in its harbor, **Mystic Seaport** (*860-572-0711; mysticseaport. org*) looks like an old port town, though one with high-end dining and interior plumbing. In this 19-acre historical wonderland you can hop onto a ship and someone will demonstrate how to climb the rigging. Poke your head into a shack and a talkative blacksmith will stress the importance of properly crafted gaff hooks. Some days there's even a band singing sea chanteys.

At the far end of the campus stands the museum's preservation pièce de résistance, a fully functional shipyard. You are welcome to tour the facility and watch the museum's crew of honest-to-God shipwrights practice their ancient craft. In 2013, they completed their greatest opus, a 5-year restoration of the *Charles W. Morgan*, the largest wooden merchant ship,

and the last wooden whaler, left afloat.

At the **Mystic Aquarium and Institute for Exploration** (*860-572-5955; mysticaquarium.org*), the welcoming committee takes the form of beluga whales swimming in outdoor pools just to the right of the entrance. Nearby Steller sea lions, northern fur seals, and a colony of more than 30 South African penguins play and frolic. Inside tanks of hypnotic jellyfish and other sea creatures, including a 1,000-square foot exhibit of more than 30 frog species. In 2017 the aquarium became one of fewer than a dozen institutions worldwide to be certified by American Humane Conservation.

If all this has you yearning to get out on the ocean, the two-masted schooner *Argia* (*860-536-0416; argiamystic.com*) offers the chance to set sail for sheltered Fishers Island Sound on a voyage that showcases islands, lighthouses, and local lore. The windjammer *Mystic Whaler* (*800-697-8420; mysticwhalercruises.com*) can whisk you out to sea for a few hours or a few days, depending on its schedule, and the strength of your sea legs.

Back in town, raw-oyster aficionados can toggle between the celebrated **Oyster Club** (*860-415-9266; oysterclubct.com*), wrapped in barn-board chic, and **S&P Oyster Co.** (*860-536-2674; sp-oyster.com*) with its wide rows of windows overlooking the river. Buttery cod is doubly warming in the brick-cozy pub at the 1754 **Captain Daniel Packer Inne** (*860-536-3555; daniel packer.com*), and seafood goes Italian at **Bravo Bravo** (*860-536-3228; bravobravo ct.com*), with linguine and clams in garlic, or champagne risotto with lobster. Once you've seen and eaten your fill for the day along the waterfront, the **Steamboat Inn** (*860-536-8300; steamboatinn.com*) is a perfect rest stop, right in the heart of the restaurants, galleries, and boutiques of downtown Mystic.

SPOTLIGHT ON

NEW ENGLAND'S ULTIMATE FALL FOLIAGE TOWN

Vermont and New Hampshire villages put up stiff competition every year for bragging rights to the best foliage town in New England—and, by extension, the world. But the pinnacle of the leaf-peeping experience can be found in the northwestern Connecticut town of **Kent** (*kentct. com*). The great foliage and the profusion of crimson and gold that leaps off the Litchfield Hills to reflect in the winding course of the Housatonic River is nothing short of breathtaking.

But the heart of the New England leaf-peeping experience lies in the accompanying details: the farm stands, covered bridges, waterfalls, and antiques stores, all framed by the colors of our most glorious season. The tiny village of Kent has all of these things in abundance, in a perfect blend of uncommon natural beauty and culture that might shame cities 10 times its size.

Only minutes away from the lovely, walkable campus of the **Kent School**, there's an artistic downtown full of bookstores and antiques, from the spare modernism of **Eckert Fine Art** (*860-592-0353; janeeckertfineart.com*) to the larger-than-life sculptures in the barnlike **R.T. Facts** (*860-927-1700; rtfacts.com*). To bring home a little of that artistic sensibility, visit **Heron American Crafts Gallery**

Macedonia Brook State Park, Kent

Aerial view of Kent

(860-927-4804; heroncraftgallery.com) for artisanal wares from around New England and beyond. While you're browsing there, try one of Kent's many inviting little eateries.

Across the Housatonic River, the hanging valley of **Macedonia Brook State Park** is carved along the side of Cobble Mountain, where Revolutionary-era residents dug iron ore out of the hills to fashion into cannonballs to fire at the British. The strenuous 7-mile blue loop trail scrambles up and down granite outcroppings, while the 3-mile orange trail offers a more relaxed hike through birches and sugar maples. The foliage is as spectacular as anywhere in New England, both close-up in the tunnel of trees along the trails, as well as in the vistas over the surrounding hills.

A more extensive homage to Kent's industrial past, the **Sloane Museum and Kent Iron Furnace** (860-927-3849; friends oftheericsloanemuseum.org), is just up Route 7, near the spectacular, tumbling multi-level **Kent Falls State Park**, where

you can follow the falls up the steep steps. If you want something more leisurely, follow the **Housatonic River Walk**, almost 5 miles of flat terrain hugging the water along the Appalachian Trail. And if biking is more your speed, check out **Kent's Bicycle Tour Company** (888-781-5368; bicycletourcompany.org). This friendly outfit will steer you toward lightly traveled byways where cars are few and postcard views are plenty.

Don't miss nearby 1700s **Mountain View Farm** (860-927-1856; moutainview farmkent.com), which boasts an enviable vista along with a bevy of organic produce. There, you can meet Maria LaFontan, who has been working with her husband, Vincent, for more than 15 years, and now tends pumpkins, squash, garlic, heirloom tomatoes, and other crops, along with raising a sizable flock of laying hens and filling jars with certified organic maple syrup. It's finds like these, after all, that epitomize the joy of leaf-peeping in New England. It's full of color, sure, but also full of surprises.

SPOTLIGHT ON
CONNECTICUT WINE TRAIL

Wine in Connecticut? You bet. Ever since the first European colonists found wild grapes growing in their new backyards, wine has been produced here. The 1897 state flag even consists of three grapevines on a silver shield, symbolizing the three colonies that became one. Under the shield appears the state motto, "Qui transtulit sustinet," meaning "What is transplanted, sustains."

However, Prohibition put a stop to this growing industry in Connecticut, and it wasn't until 1978 with the passage of the Farm Winery Act that commercial winemaking became possible again. A few pioneers proved that the environment was great for growing not only native grapes but many European varietals. This should be no surprise, since the climate is similar to northeastern France, where some of the best wines in the world are made.

Today you can find over 40 farm wineries across the state, as well as other vineyards and winemaking operations. The state of Connecticut sponsors a "passport" program, in which you can visit wineries from May to October and acquire stamps in order to enter a drawing for free vacations abroad and at home. Many of the wineries have also joined in a convenient "wine trail" (*ctwine.com*.) that provides maps, hours, and other information, as well as providing road signs and guidance in your travels from vineyard to vineyard.

In the western part of the state, some of the standouts include New Preston's **Hopkins Vineyard** (*860-868-7954; hopkinsvineyard.com*), high on a hill above Lake Waramaug. Stop in their Wine Bar Cafe on weekends to try their amazing Cabernet Francs, or attend the annual barrel tasting or harvest celebration. Up the road in Goshen, **Sunset Meadow Vineyard** (*860-201-4654; sunsetmeadowvineyards.com*) produces large amounts of estate-grown wine, and offers private events, vineyard tours, and an indoor and outdoor tasting area.

Along the Housatonic River, **Jones Family Farm** (*203-929-8425; jonesfamilyfarms.com*) in Shelton is open for wine tasting Friday through Sunday, as well as

Saltwater Farm Vineyard

A renovated WWII airplane hangar tasting room at Saltwater Farm Vineyard.

strawberry harvesting in June, blueberry picking in July and August, and a Harvest Kitchen with cooking classes.

In the Connecticut River Valley you'll find fewer wineries than in the eastern and western hills, but **Bishop's Orchards Winery and Farm Market** (*203-453-2338; bishopsorchardswinery.com*) in Guilford is open seven days a week, offering fruit wines, along with pick-your-own strawberries, blueberries, raspberries, and more. **Priam Vineyards** (*860-267-8520; priam-vineyards.com*) in Colchester offers a summer wine dinner series, tours, and a farmers market, along with some fantastic Riesling. And finally, the view from Wallingford's **Gouveia Vineyards** (*203-265-5526; gouveiavineyards.com*) never fails to take your breath away. Along with the spectacular views of central Connecticut, they offer a wine club membership, customized gift baskets, and picnicking.

In the eastern part of the state, many wineries hug the coast, but **Sharpe Hill Vineyard** (*860-974-3549; sharpehill.com*) hides in the northeastern hills of Pomfret. They offer tastings in their wine garden

and dinner in their fabulous restaurant. Even farther north is Woodstock's **Taylor Brooke Winery** (*860-974-1263; taylorbrookewinery.com*), which produces wine and a delicious brandy. High above Long Island Sound in North Stonington, **Jonathan Edwards Winery** (*860-535-0202; jedwardswinery.com*) offers an array of musical events, a gift shop, and an art gallery above the tasting room. While right on the edge of the Sound, **Saltwater Farm Vineyard** (*800-818-7258; saltwater farmvineyard.com*) has their tasting room in a vintage hangar from WWII that has been transformed into a winery and hosts private events.

The wine you will taste here will surprise you with its complexity and accessibility. If you like reds, try a chocolatey Cabernet Franc or a spicy St. Croix. For white drinkers, sample a refreshing Chardonnay or a citrusy Vidal Blanc. And, of course, many wineries also make rosés, sparkling bubblies, and sweet dessert wines. There is a wine here for every palate, and visiting a winery for a tasting is the best way to find yours. See you on the trail.

SPOTLIGHT ON

TOP 15 CONNECTICUT EVENTS

JANUARY

Sun Wine and Food Fest

Every winter Uncasville hosts a world-class celebration of food and drink at Mohegan Sun. At this feast for all your senses, rub shoulders with celebrity chefs and wine-makers and enjoy wines, craft beers, and signature dishes from New England's finest restaurants. *860-862-7779; mohegansun .com/sun-wine-and-food-fest*

MARCH

Hebron Maple Festival

This annual event takes place on Saturday and Sunday in March and features food, live music, face painting, a quilt show, and sugar house tours and demonstrations. Fill your weekend with fun, laughter and all things maple. *860-423-6389; hebron maplefest.com*

APRIL

Little Poland Festival

New Britain has one of the largest and most vibrant Polish communities on the East Coast, and their annual festival draws thousands of people to enjoy great food, fantastic entertainment, and a taste of the unique culture of Polish-Americans. *860-670-4955; littlepolandfest.com*

JUNE

International Festival of Arts and Ideas

This 15-day festival takes place primarily on the New Haven Green and includes concerts, street performers, opera, theater, and dance performances, along with lectures and discussions that focus on everything from food to international politics. In addition to the lectures and performances, there are walking tours of New Haven led by experts, food tours through the excellent New Haven restaurants, and more. *888-278-4332; artidea.org*

Sea Music Festival

Mystic Seaport hosts performers from around the globe who carry on the classic musical traditions of the Golden Age of Sail. Performers sing sea chanteys and other music from the maritime cultures of the United Kingdom, Italy, the Netherlands, France, Canada, and Africa. *860-572-0711; mystic seaport.org*

Sunken Garden Poetry Festival

One of the country's premier poetry venues, the Sunken Garden Poetry Festival takes place Wednesday evenings every summer in Farmington. Lawn chairs and picnic blankets spread out in front of the majestic pillars of Hill-stead Museum's white mansion, and the sunken gardens' topiary bushes and manicured hedges frame the gazebo where artists perform. *860-677-4787; hillstead.org*

JULY

Deep River Ancient Muster

This event has set records for being the largest of its kind in the world, with dozens of fife and drum corps from all over the nation and Europe parading up Main Street in Deep River. Afterward, head to Devitt Field to watch evening performances and check out vendors selling fifes, drums, music, hats, and more. The event is free, though it may cost you to park. The nearby Museum of Fife and Drum is full of uniforms, performance gear, musical instruments, and photographs. *860-767-2237; companyoffifeanddrum.org*

Litchfield Jazz Festival

The western hills' epic jazz fest lasts from midday through the evening hours on Saturday and Sunday on a summer weekend. Usually there are over a thousand seats, but thousands more eager listeners sprawl on picnic blankets and lawn chairs throughout the meadows. *860-361-6285; litchfieldjazzfest.com*

Sailfest

This 3-day festival brings 300,000 people into downtown New London. There's a road race, fireworks, a lobster dinner, fine arts and crafts vendors, cruises in the harbor, a beer tent, food vendors, a temporary amusement park for the kids, and the sails that give the festival its name, with a tall ship or three to tour on the docks downtown. *860-444-1879; sailfest.org*

Westport Fine Arts Festival

There are a number of fine arts festivals throughout Connecticut in the summer, but Westport's reputation as a home for both the rich and artistic brings out real talent every year. It's been around for almost 40 years, and usually features around 150 artists displaying their work along the Westport River and in the squares of this lovely town. *203-505-8716; westportdma.com /events-fine-arts-festival*

AUGUST

Podunk Bluegrass Music Festival

Some of the finest local and national bluegrass groups descend on Hebron's Lions Fairgrounds to perform. Check out the workshops, traditional crafts, storytelling, jam sessions, a variety of food, and an entertainment and activities area for the kids. Bring your instrument—some say the best parts of this festival are the pick-up jam sessions in the fields. *860-828-9818; podunkbluegrass.org*

SEPTEMBER

Durham Fair

Begun in 1916, the largest agricultural fair in Connecticut takes place on the Durham Town Green and the adjoining fields, with antiques; seminars on food, farming, and garden care; animal pulls; baked and canned goods; crafts; needlework; photography; plants; flowers; fruit; and giant pumpkins. If these traditional fair events are not enough, there's also a demolition derby, a truck pull, a carousel, midway rides, and more. *860-349-9495; durhamfair.com*

Norwalk Oyster Festival

Since 1978 people have been coming to Norwalk the weekend after Labor Day to celebrate (and eat) the mighty oyster. You can prove your oyster-eating prowess in a "slurp-off" contest, or just enjoy old oyster boats, a shucking contest, marching bands, harbor cruises, arts and crafts exhibitions, and more. *203-838-9444; seaport.org*

OCTOBER

Harwinton Fair

Connecticut has many town fairs, but not many that have been going steadily since 1853. The Harwinton Fair is one of the largest fairs as well, with hundreds of attractions, from skillet tossing and pig racing to demonstrations of pioneer and Civil War living. The fair hosts a large traveling carnival with rides, a high-wire act by circus performers, and dozens of craft and food vendors. *860-485-0464; harwintonfair.com*

DECEMBER

Old Saybrook Torchlight Parade

In colonial New England, Saybrook's village militia would muster during early December and march to the town green carrying torches and lanterns, and the rest of the townspeople followed, all joining in a carol sing. The revival today in Old Saybrook is much the same, with dozens of fife and drum corps marching and playing, filling the cold air with merriment. *860-388-3266; oldsaybrookchamber.com*

RHODE ISLAND

THE OCEAN STATE

———o———

Though measuring a mere thousand square miles or so, New England's littlest state packs a lot of appeal—and as its nickname suggests, much of that allure is concentrated along its 400 miles of coastline. Sparkling Narragansett Bay is a top adventure destination that calls to sailors, kayakers, and surfers. At the head of the bay, the capital city of Providence hums with art and culture and a nationally recognized dining scene; meanwhile, its famed neighbor to the south, Newport, sits on the water like a sleek super-yacht, with its Gilded Age mansions and world-renowned cliff walk. And tucked into the southeastern corner of the state is the Farm Coast, a picturesque collection of rural villages whose vineyards, restaurants, farm stands, and markets showcase the bounty of field and sea.

Even when you head inland for your adventures, you're never far from Rhode Island's refreshing waters. Maybe that's why its historic cities always seem in the flow of what's trending and thought-provoking. It's worth noting, too, that the state's capital has a magical glitter on evenings when water meets another essential element to create WaterFire, a spectacle that enchants like nothing else. This is Rhode Island, shining bright.

RHODE ISLAND ESSENTIALS

PROVIDENCE & NORTH

BREAKTIME BOWL & BAR, PAWTUCKET

Invented in Massachusetts in the 1890s, duckpin bowling uses small, palm-sized balls with no finger holes. The last surviving industrial duckpin bowling alley was built in Pawtucket for Hope Webbing millworkers' entertainment around 1920. Today, the six remarkably preserved lanes of this unique bowling alley echo once again with the clatter of short, squat pins. In the evenings, Breaktime morphs into the ultimate throwback hangout, with pub food and a full bar. Rolling a strike is pure joy, for everyone except the people who have to set up the pins by hand after every round. *401-427-7006; breaktimebowlandbar.com*

Scenes from Breaktime Bowl & Bar

BROWN & HOPKINS COUNTRY STORE, CHEPACHET

Out in the northwest hills of Rhode Island, in the middle of a large forest, the charming village of Chepachet features the oldest continuously operating country store in the nation. You can explore two floors of goodies, from furnishings to clothing to dolls. You'll find 1803® candles, homespun fabrics by the yard, and gourmet treats. Don't miss the candy treats like Mary Janes and Squirrel Nut Zippers that generations before you have always enjoyed. *401-568-4830; brownandhopkins.com*

CRUISING THE BLACKSTONE RIVER

The Blackstone River runs from Providence to Worcester, Massachusetts. It once powered Pawtucket's Slater Mill, the first successful water-powered textile factory in America. But the Blackstone paid a price for its fame: Years of industrial waste polluted it beyond recognition. Today this clean, dynamic river has been resurrected and named a National Heritage Corridor, home to turtles and herons. You can

Kayaking the Blackstone River

tour it aboard the 40-passenger *Blackstone Valley Explorer* riverboat, or on the exclusive *Samuel Slater*, an authentic British canal boat that provides overnight accommodations as a B&B. *401-724-2200; rivertourblackstone.com*

Slater Mill

CULINARY ARTS MUSEUM AT JOHNSON & WALES UNIVERSITY, PROVIDENCE

In diner lingo, a "splash of red noise" is tomato soup, and "burn the British" is a toasted English muffin—just the tip of the iceberg of gastronomic information you'll discover at this endlessly fascinating museum. Its carefully curated collection showcases the varied elements of cooking and cuisine across five centuries. Perhaps you'll find yourself drawn to the collection of fine service pieces and cutlery, including silver sandwich boxes, knife rests, and egg guillotines. The humble early New England kitchen, with its glowing hearth filled with hanging cast-iron pots, reminds us both how much cuisine has changed, and how much it has stayed the same. *401-598-2805; culinary.org*

FEDERAL HILL FOOD TOUR, PROVIDENCE

Dubbed the "Little Italy" of Providence, Federal Hill has always been known as the culinary heartbeat of the city, the place to find mom-and-pop restaurants serving homemade pasta with a sublime tomato sauce. Who better to show you around these streets than a local pastry chef who taught at Johnson & Wales University? On this three-hour walking tour, award winning chef, Cindy Salvato will regale you with the history of the neighborhood while stopping at landmarks such as Scialo Bros. Bakery, which recently celebrated its centennial; Costantino's Venda Ravioli, an Italian food emporium known for its pastas and sauces; and Gasbarro's Wines, in business since 1898. *800-656-0713; savoringrhodeisland.com*

(Above) This late 19th-century photo captures a re-created scene of everyday life, as women washed and dried dishes for the studio camera. (Left) This 1933 cookbook is one of many carefully preserved pieces in the Culinary Arts Museum's collection.

Restaurants on Atwells Avenue, in the heart of Federal Hill.

MODERN DINER, PAWTUCKET

Set in a red-and-cream-colored Sterling Streamliner, shaped like a locomotive, and manufactured in the early 1940s in Merrimac, Massachusetts, the Modern holds the distinction of being the very first diner named to the National Register of Historic Places. Its food also makes it one of the top diners of any vintage in New England. Be warned, though: the line outside the door on Saturday mornings has been considerably longer since the Food Network named the Modern's custard French toast the best diner dish in the country. *401-726-8390; moderndinerri.com*

A PawSox pitcher winds up for the pitch.

> **TRAVEL TIP:** Careful—ordering coffee "regular" in Rhode Island (and often in nearby states) will get you one with cream and sugar.

PAWTUCKET RED SOX, PAWTUCKET

Perhaps no other minor league team in New England has captured the hearts of fans like the PawSox. This is where the Boston team really begins; Nomar, Roger Clemens, and Jim Rice all remember their early days at McCoy Stadium. One of the most

Retro interior of the Modern Diner

Providence skyline

striking features of this ballpark is seeing the murals of the famous players during their time in Pawtucket. The longest game in baseball history was played here April 18, 1981, against young Cal Ripkin, Jr. and his Rochester Red Wings. It went on and on for an astonishing 33 innings. *401-724-7300; pawsox.com*

PROSPECT TERRACE PARK, PROVIDENCE

This public park boasts a breathtaking panorama from its perch high on College Hill. Stand by the memorial to Providence Plantation founder Roger Williams, and the heart of Rhode Island's capital city spreads out below you like a banquet. You can see the steeples of the old town, the skyscrapers of Downcity, and the regal dome of the state house. Come here on a clear evening and watch the most beautiful sunsets in New England set the glass and granite facades of Providence ablaze.

RISD MUSEUM, PROVIDENCE

Rhode Island School of Design features a museum with an aggressively diverse collection, in order to expose its students to many artistic styles. The Benefit Street building houses more than 86,000 objects —including furniture, textiles, art, silver, and more. The permanent collection includes local highlights like 18th-century Newport furniture makers Goddard and Townsend as well as 19th-century Rhode Island painters John Noble Barlow and Gilbert Stuart. But you'll find all the big names here, too, including Monet, Manet,

TRAVEL TIP: Head to Gilbert Stuart's Birthplace and Museum in Saunderstown and learn about the painter who immortalized the heroes of the American Revolution.

(Top left and center) The RISD Museum is home to a diverse collection of furniture, sculptures, textiles, and more. (Below) Enjoy the flickering lights and enchanting atmosphere of WaterFire Providence.

WaterFire Providence

Roger Williams Park

Picasso, and Warhol. Don't miss Winslow Homer's dramatic *On a Lee Shore*, which captures the Maine coast so exquisitely we think it's reason enough to schedule a visit. 401-709-8402; risdmuseum.org

ROGER WILLIAMS PARK BOTANICAL CENTER, PROVIDENCE

Located in Victorian-era Roger Williams Park, when this plant-lover's paradise opened in 2007 it became the largest garden conservatory in New England. With 23,000 square feet of greenhouse space, the center is home to more than 150 species of tropical and subtropical plants, with palm trees, waterfalls, orchids, cacti, and many other exotic blooms and fragrances. After you've browsed the flora, take in some fauna at the park's zoo, ride the carousel, and enjoy this rare historical gem to the fullest. *401-785-9450; providenceri.gov/botanical-center/*

WATERFIRE PROVIDENCE

More than 10 million people have seen WaterFire Providence—Barnaby Evans's magnificent installation of 100 bonfires at the heart of the city. And no wonder—it is one of the best free summer events in New England. There are evening lightings of the fires throughout the year. Stroll through the enchanted flickering lights along the three rivers, listen to haunting music in the night air, and wonder at mysterious boats gliding through the darkness. *401-273-1155; waterfire.org*

> **TRAVEL TIP:** Interested in Revolutionary history? Check out the Coventry homestead of George Washington's right-hand man, Nathanael Greene.

EAST BAY & NEWPORT

AMARAL'S FISH AND CHIPS, WARREN

Are you wondering what all the fuss is about when it comes to Rhode Island stuffies, those stuffed and baked quahogs? Well, head on over to Amaral's for the delicious answer. This family-owned eatery in up-and-coming Warren prides itself on letting the seafood shine through. Delectable clams are shucked and chopped fresh daily, seasoned, and baked in a hot oven until they get that special, crisp-on-top texture. *401-247-0675; amaralsfishandchips.com*

AMERICA'S CUP CHARTERS, NEWPORT

You can't go to Rhode Island without experiencing the state's nautical side. A perfect way to do that is with a three-hour sail aboard an authentic America's Cup yacht. The boats include the *Nefertiti*, the 1970 winner *Weatherly*, the *American Eagle*, best known as Ted Turner's stepping stone to America's Cup victory, and the *Intrepid*, which was the last classic wooden yacht to defend the Cup, in 1970. You could be chosen to be a timekeeper, mainsheet handler, or primary grinder, which involves turning a winch as fast as possible so that the foresail can change direction. *401-846-9886; americascupcharters.com*

BLITHEWOLD MANSION, BRISTOL

One of New England's most intensely planted and lovingly tended landscapes, Blithewold's thirty-three acres of gardens, lawns, specimen trees, and rare and unusual plants are equal parts historic treasure and living classroom. True to the early-1900s vision of owner Bessie Van Wickle McKee and landscape architect John De Wolf, this Narragansett Bay estate inspires those who work with nature and those who simply relish watching it unfold. Enjoy its exotic abundance for both summer concerts and Christmas celebrations. *401-253-2707; blithewold.org*

Amaral's Fish & Chips

CLIFF WALK, NEWPORT

In 1975 Newport's fabled Cliff Walk was the first public path in New England to be designated a National Recreation Trail, but it had already been famous for over a century. It winds its way along Aquidneck's cliffs past some of Newport's most impressive and historic mansions above the rocky shore. Walk the same path that the Vanderbilts, the Astors, and Henry and William James walked, but watch out for the steep drop offs into the crashing Atlantic. *401-845-5300; cliffwalk.com*

COLT STATE PARK, BRISTOL

Just outside of Bristol is Colt State Park, 464 acres open to the sweep of Narragansett Bay. Once owned by Samuel P. Colt, nephew to the Colt arms manufacturer, it's now a place for tossing a Frisbee, walking the verdant trails, or picnicking on the long, manicured lawns. The East Bay Bike Path runs past the park, and a quick turn yields an additional four miles of trails. If the sea calls, it's probably only the seabirds cruising overhead, letting you know who really owns the park. *401-253-7482; riparks.com*

America's Cup Charters

Blithewold Mansion Garden

Cliff Walk, Newport

TRAVEL TIP: If you're driving over the Claiborne Pell Bridge between Newport and Jamestown, have a passenger ready to take photos of the spectacular views from the top.

EAST BAY BIKE PATH, BRISTOL TO PROVIDENCE

Sights, sounds, and scents of the bay accompany your walk or ride along this former railbed of the Providence/Worcester line. Stretching 14.5 miles along the shore from Independence Park in Bristol to India Point Park in Providence, this popular path is the keystone of a huge network of bike lanes and trails throughout Rhode Island. Possible stops include a Crescent Park carousel ride, wildlife watching at Audubon's Environmental Education Center, and Del's frozen lemonade at Colt State Park. *401-222-2450; dot.ri.gov/community/bikeri*

GREEN ANIMALS TOPIARY GARDEN, PORTSMOUTH

Bonsai shrubs are green with envy over the Green Animals Topiary Garden. Sculpted from yew, California privet, and English boxwood, these trees and bushes take geometric forms and animal shapes, from a giraffe to a teddy bear. The oldest topiary property in the country also has vegetable and herb gardens, orchards, and a grand Victorian house overlooking Narragansett Bay. *401-847-1000; newportmansions.org*

INTERNATIONAL TENNIS HALL OF FAME, NEWPORT

In a city filled with "look, but don't touch" attractions, this architecturally magnificent sports shrine engages an interactive generation. Gutted to the walls for a complete overhaul, the hall reopened in 2015 with vibrant galleries and multimedia marvels. Brimming with more than 1,900 artifacts of tennis history (including Andy Roddick's red, white, and blue sneakers and Rene Lacoste's original "crocodile" blazer), this museum is perfect for sports fanatics. But it appeals to families, too, with interactive exhibits such as a touch table that lets visitors "serve" tennis trivia questions back and forth, and a "Call the Match" exhibit in which anyone can step into the role of a big-league sports broadcaster. Plus, you can participate in clinics or book time on the grass courts where 1881's first U.S. National Lawn Tennis Championships were played. *401-849-3990; tennisfame.com*

A menagerie of animals can be found at the Green Animals Topiary Garden.

THE FARM COAST

A tiny part of a tiny state, Rhode Island's Farm Coast can be driven in less than an hour. On a map, the region stretches from Tiverton down to Little Compton, then east into Massachusetts, to include Westport and Dartmouth. Farmers and fishermen have staked claim to the land for generations, and as you travel through this picturesque countryside, your eye swivels from produce stands, to bales of hay glinting in the sun, to sailboats on the seascape of Narragansett Bay.

Today, artists and craftspeople have also claimed a niche, and it is no surprise, with landscape as art everywhere you look. You'll find beauty in tiny Tiverton Four Corners, with restored 18th-century buildings clustered around a crossroads, and

Little Compton, widely regarded as the prettiest town in the state. As you come upon that village, past undulating farms, the road twists around a white church, through a "downtown" made up of a century-old general store and a tidy library, to a restaurant by the town commons famous for its chowder and Jonny Cakes. And along the water you'll find **South Shore Beach** and **Goosewing Beach**, broad sandy stretches filled with sunbathers and surfers on hot summer days.

Just across the state line in Massachusetts, **Westport Point** is a historic fishing community filled with houses from the 1700s that tumble toward the harbor. You'll find lines out the door for **Revolution Lobster**'s daily specials, with fish caught just hours before by a boat docked next to the restaurant patio. Just beyond to the east, **Horseneck Beach State Park** will surprise you with its rolling dunes and a 1.5-mile paved walking path by the water. Drive even further through winding country roads, past farms and gorgeous stone walls, and you'll come to **Demarest Lloyd State Park**—rarely crowded, and filled with beach roses.

For those who like wine, these microclimates are also home to several vineyards, so look for signs following the **Coastal Wine Trail**. But with or without a sip of the grape, the Farm Coast is a magical place, with quiet beaches, charming villages, and miles of fields golden in the sun. *401-635-4664; farmcoast.com*

The fertile Farm Coast yields crops and farm products of all kinds, which are showcased at welcoming local shops such as Milk & Honey (top left) in Tiverton Four Corners.

The design of Vernon Court is rumored to have been loosely based on the 18th-century French mansion, Château d'Haroué. Today it is home to the National Museum of American Illustration.

W.C. Weyth's The Doryman (The Lobsterman) *is one of many works featured in the National Museum of American Illustration's "American Imagist" collection.*

NATIONAL MUSEUM OF AMERICAN ILLUSTRATION, NEWPORT

Architecturally splendid Vernon Court may look like a typical Newport Mansion, but it is actually a living, evolving estate that reflects the passions of owners and directors Laurence and Judy Goffman Cutler. Chief among those passions is exhibiting their incredible collection of masterpieces by beloved American illustrators such as Norman Rockwell and Maxfield Parrish. Here, these remarkably relatable commercial images get their due as both art and a chronicle of American culture. Don't miss the creative works of Mother Nature outside, including the champion trees within the museum's Frederick Law Olmsted Park and Arboretum. *401-851-8949; american illustration.org*

ROSE ISLAND LIGHTHOUSE, NEWPORT

If you've ever fantasized about sleeping in a lighthouse, you're in luck. At Rose Island Light in Narragansett Bay's East Passage you can stay in the first-floor museum bedrooms overnight or spend a week's working vacation in the keeper's quarters upstairs. On the National Register of Historic Places, this 1871 house and light tower was abandoned in 1970 after nearly a century of use. It was later restored to become one of the state's most authentic and charming destinations. Arrive by ferry, sleep surrounded by the sea, awaken to gulls chattering and seals barking, and teach the kids about washbowls and pitcher pumps. *401-847-4242; roseisland.org*

TOURO SYNAGOGUE, NEWPORT

Dedicated in 1763, America's oldest standing Jewish synagogue is a reminder that Colonial Newport not only tolerated this religious minority, but also welcomed its

Touro Synagogue

members into the ranks of its prosperous citizens. The Georgian architecture and stately interior add to the allure of this site, which is on the National Register of Historic Places. Most of the 35,000 annual visitors are impressed by the building itself and the 500-year-old deerskin Torah housed there. But perhaps even more impressive is the way the synagogue still speaks to the enduring American dream. *401-847-4794; tourosynagogue.org*

Rose Island Lighthouse

→ NEWPORT MANSIONS

In the late nineteenth century, wealthy industrialists from America's growing cities needed a place to spend their summers, and the rocky promontory at the southern tip of Newport provided the perfect spot, breezy and cool, with views of the Atlantic on three sides. The new colony of wealthy builders held garden parties and ballroom dances, and engaged in social and architectural one-upmanship. This habit of keeping-up-with-the-Vanderbilts resulted in larger, grander, and more expensive houses, or "white elephants," as author Henry James called them. The owners referred to them diffidently as summer "cottages," but they knew perfectly well that they were creating grand palaces for a new American aristocracy that was short on heritage but long on currency.

If you see only one of these mansions during a visit to Newport, make it **The Breakers**, completed in 1892. The sprawling 70-room, 13-acre, Renaissance-inspired

The Breakers

estate of railroad tycoon Cornelius Vanderbilt II boasts gold- and platinum-covered walls, unmatched detailing, a 2½-story great hall, and a glorious view of the Atlantic.

Just to the southwest you'll find **Rosecliff**, considered by many to be the most beautiful, or at least the most romantic, of the mansions. Built in 1902, the sweeping H-shaped French pavilion was designed specifically for entertaining, and its famous 3,200-square-foot ballroom has been featured in such films as *The Great Gatsby*, *27 Dresses*, *Amistad*, and *True Lies*.

Next door is the 1892 **Marble House**, another Vanderbilt mansion styled after the Grand and Petit Trianons of Versailles and built with some 500,000 cubic feet of creamy marble. The interior includes a salon where every surface is covered in 22-karat gold, while on the back lawn a charming Chinese teahouse overlooks the sea.

Among the other spectacular mansions you can explore are **the Elms**, with its extensive formal gardens; **Belcourt Castle**, with a distinctly medieval feel; and **Rough Point**, the Newport home of heiress Doris Duke, filled with a remarkable collection of French furniture, European art, Chinese porcelains, and Turkish carpets.

The mansions of Newport are lasting reminders of conspicuous consumption in Gilded-Age America, and one of the wonders of New England. They defy expectations, and often defy imagination. But they are very real, and better yet, they are waiting for you. *newportmansions.org; newportrestoration.org*

Rosecliff

The Elms

WHITE HORSE TAVERN, NEWPORT

History buffs and bar aficionados alike will want to put the White Horse on their bucket list. It first opened its doors in 1673, making it the oldest watering hole in the United States, and since that time it has wined, dined, and warmed generations of guests in front of its four working fireplaces. Elegant dinners, cozy Sunday brunches, seafood direct from the docks and house-made charcuterie round out a menu that also includes the basics of burgers and beers. Come hungry and prepare to soak up the well-preserved colonial aura. *401-849-3600; whitehorsenewport.com*

(Below) Dine the way your colonial fore-fathers did at the beautifully preserved White Horse Tavern. After three centuries, the menu is perfect!

WEST BAY & SOUTH

CAMP CRONIN, NARRAGANSETT

When the sands of Narragansett's town and state beaches start filling up with crowds in the summertime, savvy locals tote their beach chairs to this tucked-away beach off Ocean Road. Sure, this state-owned fishing area doesn't boast huge, surf-ready waves, and the toilets are the portable kind, but it doesn't cost a penny to play in saltwater here. The sunsets and the heart-stirring view of Point Judith Light will be worth the small trouble finding this hidden gem.

(Top center) Camp Cronin boasts gorgeous vistas and tranquil beach walks. (Below) Don't miss a visit to Point Judith Light.

(From left) Ocean House and its Seaside Terrace

DINING AT OCEAN HOUSE, WATCH HILL

Following a five-year, $140 million facelift, this Victorian grand dame once again reigns as one of the most luxurious over-nights on the Rhode Island coast. However, you don't need to have the deep pockets of a Vanderbilt or Astor to enjoy a taste of the good life. This five-star hotel's many excellent on-site dining options are open to visitors as well as guests, making this one of our favorite spots for a memorable sea-side lunch—especially when you're sitting on the glorious wraparound verandah. *855-678-0364; oceanhouseri.com*

FLYING HORSE CAROUSEL, WATCH HILL

In the Victorian-era seaside village of Watch Hill, the Flying Horse Carousel claims to be *one* of the nation's oldest car-ousels, built around 1867. To claim the top spot outright would risk a battle to the death with a carousel on Martha's Vine-yard. However, this is probably the nation's last surviving example of the "flying horses" model, which means that its hand-carved wooden steeds are not attached to poles that go up and down. Instead, they hang suspended from a center frame, causing them to fly out when the carousel

turns. The ride is for kids only, but the spectacle is free for all to enjoy. *401-348-6007; watchhillbeachandcarousel.com*

MATUNUCK OYSTER BAR, EAST MATUNUCK

The New England oyster industry is on the rebound, and in recent years Rhode Island's shellfish farms have earned some serious bragging rights. At Matunuck Oyster Bar, Perry Raso's popular water-front bar, you can slurp up worthy gems like Moonstones, Bear Points, Cedar Islands, and Aquidnecks, all sold in rota-tion. The star attractions, though, are the Mantunuck oysters that Raso cultivates just a stone's throw away, in a saltwater basin off Long Island Sound. Their hyper-local flavor comes through in a distinct briny crispness and lightly sweet finish, like a friendly good-bye. *401-783-4202; rhodyoysters.com*

NAPATREE POINT, WATCH HILL

With its highest point at a mere 812 feet, Rhode Island is not a place you might think of when you want to take a hike. Yet it does have some of the longest beach strolls in New England, including Napatree Point, which juts out from the village of Watch Hill. Take off your shoes and listen to the waves as you saunter along a wild

→ RHODE ISLAND'S REGIONAL TREATS

If you're eating breakfast in Rhode Island, be sure to ask for a plate of **Jonny Cakes**. These corn-based pancakes seem simple, but are actually the subject of hot debates. Did they originate with the Native Americans or the settlers? Do you grind whitecap flint or white dent corn for meal, and how do you do it? How do you even spell the name: journey-cake, Johnny cake, or Jonny cake? Some of these arguments have even gone to the state legislature, with the thick, boiling-water method of South County fighting it out with the thin, cold-milk method of Newport County over which method was superior/correct. Best not to get involved, and just bring a healthy appetite.

The legislature had a similar argument over the official state drink in 1993, with Del's Frozen Lemonade from Cranston narrowly losing to the more widespread **Coffee Milk**. This chocolate-milk-like beverage is built by mixing instant coffee with sugar and corn syrup. This concoction is then bottled and added, a few spoonfuls at a time, to a glass of milk, then stirred and enjoyed. You can also add vanilla ice cream and blend the whole thing together into a **Coffee Cabinet**—more familiarly called a *frappe* by other New Englanders, and a *milkshake* by those from beyond.

Although you'll find many versions of stuffed clams around New England, it's only in Li'l Rhody that they're called **Stuffies**. There are as many ways to make this seafood treat as there are delis, pizza shops, grocery stores, seafood shacks, fish markets, and upscale eateries to make them. However, the basic recipe includes breadcrumbs, diced quahogs, and spices baked on the half-shell. Some stuffie cooks add chopped onion, celery, and sweet or hot peppers; some spice the mix like Thanksgiving stuffing; others make a Portuguese stew, complete with *chouriço* sausage. Still others swear that true stuffed clams should taste only like chopped quahogs and clam-juice-soaked bread. You can add hot sauce or lemon juice on top, until you become a purist like the other locals.

Sunset at Watch Hill

strip of coastline all the way to the point of this crescent-shaped beach, enjoying views of Connecticut and Fishers Island. On the return trip, you'll be treated to a view of the Victorian houses that cling to the bluffs of Watch Hill. *visitwatchhill.com*

SUNRISE AT BEAVERTAIL LIGHTHOUSE, JAMESTOWN

Is there a more dramatic place to watch the sunrise than from the rocky shores of Beavertail State Park? Get to the cozy island town of Jamestown, Rhode Island before dawn, and reward yourself for getting up early with a steaming cup of coffee and a warm muffin at James- town Harbor's East Ferry Market & Deli (*401-423-3270; jamestownri.com/efdeli*).

Then head south to the 1856 Beavertail Lighthouse for one of the most dramatic sunrises in America. *beavertaillight.org*

SURFING AT TOWN BEACH, NARRAGANSETT

Town Beach in Narragansett is a nice beach to sit on and soak in the rays. But when there are storms over the Atlan- tic, the swells get gnarly, and the surfers come out in droves. You can surf this section of Narragansett year-round, but from mid-July to mid-September the crescent-shaped beach and shifting sandbars often produce waves in excess of ten feet. Bring your own board or rent one from any number of local outfitters. *narragansettri.com*

(Left) Beavertail Lighthouse (Above) Narragansett Bay surfing

SPOTLIGHT ON
BLOCK ISLAND

In colonial times, Block Island earned the nickname "Bermuda of the North" thanks to its habit of luring wayward ships onto treacherous shoals. In response, the first lighthouse was built in 1829, and in the two centuries since, improvements in modern navigation technology have made it less hazardous to approach. Yet one thing hasn't changed—it remains a perfect island on which to be marooned, especially in the middle of summer.

This 7,000-acre paradise is situated a dozen miles off the coast of Rhode Island, and is deemed a "last great place" by the Nature Conservancy. More importantly for visitors, it manages to balance an air of sophistication without being haughty or off-putting in the least. You'll find a smattering of Victorian-era hotels and tidy bed-and-breakfasts, but it's not a bustling place, nor is it the sort that feels compelled to puff itself up to impress visitors. The status of summer residents tends to be measured not by the square footage of their homes but by how well they know the island's network of walking trails, or how many of the 150 species of migrating birds they can identify.

Take the hour-long ferry ride from the village of Galilee and you'll disembark onto a pork chop–shaped island where weathered houses perch on hillsides, bordered by old stone walls and blue-green ponds. This is **Old Harbor** in New Shoreham, the only town on the island. Walking up Water Street and beyond you'll find thoroughfares lined with gabled hotels, terraced restaurants, a few shops, and ice cream parlors.

Those of you interested in the history of this fascinating island, head to the **Block Island Historical Society Museum** (*401-466-2481; blockislandhistorical.org*), located in a former inn dating back to 1871. But the island is better known for its

more leisurely activities, its quiet walks, and its lounge-worthy beaches. The best way to explore the island is a 13-mile bicycle jaunt around the ring roads. Head south on Spring Street, and after leaving town you'll reach **Southeast Lighthouse** (*401-466-5009*), which stands on the highest ground of any light in New England. Stroll around the structure, then head west to the Mohegan Bluffs parking lot. One trail leads along the majestic bluffs; another leads down to a beach, far below the massive walls of rock.

As for the beaches, pick one to suit your mood. A grand beach to start your day is the three-mile-long **Crescent Beach**, sometimes called Town Beach, where the sunning and leisurely walking are equally appealing. Farther north along Corn Neck Road **Mansion Beach** promises the best

waves for body surfing on the island. It is named for the mansion built by Mrs. Edward Searles in the 1890s, but today all you'll find is a giant stone foundation. The building burned in 1963.

Block Island is perfect for a day trip, but should you make a weekend of it, look to **Hotel Manisses** (*401-466-9898; hotelmanisses.com*), with its Victorian ambience and sophisticated dining. Or try its family-friendly sister property, the **1661 Inn**. On a hilltop over the harbor, the **Atlantic Inn** (*401-466-5883; atlanticinn.com*) has hosted guests since 1879. In keeping with that 19th-century atmosphere, you'll find no televisions in its twenty-one guestrooms, just water views and sea breezes. And if you have a pup in tow, the beach-chic **Darius Inn** (*401-466-2722; dariusblockisland.com*) offers five first-floor suites for four-legged guests and their owners.

Keep an eye out for "treasure"—specifically, the glass orbs that artist Eben Horton has been hiding all over the island for the past few summers. You might find them in washed-up lobster pots, in restaurant flowerbeds, and even in the community garden's composter. It's a simple game with an irresistible hook: The floats might be anywhere, and if you find one, you get to keep it.

Block Island Lighthouse

SPOTLIGHT ON
DINING AROUND PROVIDENCE

Providence is a small city in the country's most diminutive state, but it has punches far above its weight when it comes to cultural relevance, art scene, and restaurants. In fact, Providence consistently ranks near the top for having the most restaurants per capita in America.

You'll find some distinguished, enduring, and worthy restaurants here, like **Al Forno, Gracie's**, and **Bacaro**. And there are plenty of homegrown cheap eats to choose from, too, like **Mike's Kitchen** pizza, **Haven Brothers** burgers, and **Olneyville New York System**'s hot dogs with special sauce. But we recommend that you also seek out the little independent bistros whose ambition and gumption seems to match that of the city itself.

Cozy as a speakeasy, **North** (*401-421-1100; foodbynorth.com*) offers creative cocktails and a pan-Asian menu that layers together sweet, sour, buttery, and umami flavors. Even desserts have a savory note, like cider doughnuts with fresh thyme. The roasted chicken ramen feels as comforting as Grandma's chicken and dumplings. Two blocks away is **The Grange** (*401-831-0600; providencegrange .com*), a homey vegetarian restaurant that somehow manages to please everyone, even carnivores. For dinner, try the pierogi with potatoes and kimchi.

Just to the west is the terrific **Nick's on Broadway** (*401-421-0286; nickson broadway.com*) with its famous brunch. Try the house-made brioche French toast, or baked local polenta with eggs, cheddar, and greens. Then for dinner head across I-95 to downtown's **Birch** (*401-272-3105; birchrestaurant.com*), for a specialist

seasonal menu, and modern prix-fixe dining. The space is tiny and the service is personal. Don't miss anything made with the unusual ingredients that chef-owner Benjamin Sukle loves, like sea beans, amaranth, or beach plums.

Just to the east near the School of Design is **New Rivers** (*401-751-0350; newriversrestaurant.com*). Inspired by local bounty, chef-owner Beau Vestal has brought new life to a Providence institution. The house-made charcuterie is a year-round favorite; the seasonal dishes we love have included pork belly with figs, cider, and Dijon. And on the south side of the university complexes is **Persimmon** (*401-432-7422; persimmonri.com*), where chef-owner Champe Speidel changes his menu based on what's being harvested at the farms. A meal might include New England lamb rillettes, beignets made with local greens, and corn bisque, or could feature a spectacular bowl of homemade pasta with sweet peas and lobster.

SPOTLIGHT ON

THE GREAT NEW ENGLAND CLAMBAKE

The pleasures of a real New England clambake—the authentic kind that begins with a pit in the sand and ends with smoky shellfish dipped in butter—are always burnished by a patina of history and heritage. Here is a return to life as it used to be: a simple, elemental meal enjoyed outdoors, preferably in view of the ocean.

There's real heritage to back up this nostalgia, as shellfish bakes have long been the tradition of Wampanoag, Wabanaki, and other Northeast native tribes. Clambakes as a social event, though, didn't take root until the late 1700s, when the Old Colony Club in Plymouth, Massachusetts, hosted a "Forefathers' Day" feast, with a menu of oysters, succotash, clams, and apple pie. Over time, this annual event came to be known as the "Feast of the Shells."

As leisure travel to the coast became more accessible in the 19th century, the New England clambake achieved ubiquity. In a method that hasn't changed much over the centuries, some hardy souls dig a pit on a beach, preferably near some clamming beds, and line it with rocks. A wood fire is set ablaze on the rocks, burned down to coals, and then raked away. With the rocks giving off ample heat, the pit is layered with seaweed to lend steam *and* smoke. The food is added, usually some combination of clams, mussels, lobsters, corn, potatoes, and smoky meat like bacon or chouriço. A wet tarp laid over the top creates a permeable "lid." After 90 minutes or so, the tarp is pulled away and the feast begins, with drawn butter, bibs, and lots of napkins at the ready.

In 1888, a group of Quakers in Dartmouth, Massachusetts, hosted their first Allen's Neck Friends Meeting Clambake (*508-994-5816; neym.org*), a tradition that continues to this day on the third Thursday in August. The town of Carver, Massachusetts, has been hosting a massive community clambake every July since 1901 during its annual **Old Home Day** (*carveroldhomeday.org*). Other clambakes are exclusively commercial enterprises, though no less traditional: Caterers like **Woodman's** (*800-649-1773; woodmans.com*) of Essex, Massachusetts, and **Cabbage Island Clambakes** (*207-633-7200; cabbageislandclambakes*) near Boothbay, Maine, pull off feasts all summer long for paying customers. On Cape Cod, meanwhile, the **Chatham Bars Inn** (*800-527-4884; chathambarsinn.com*) puts the emphasis on local sourcing for its summer clambake dinners, with the seafood pulled from the waters around Chatham and the produce grown at its own farm.

Rhode Island, too, has plenty of clambakes worth seeking out. Events like the **Rose Island Lighthouse Clambake** (*401-847-4242; roseislandlighthouse.org*) occur regularly throughout the warmer months at numerous locations around the state. The most acclaimed place in the state to experience this tradition might be the 1875 **Castle Hill Inn** (*401-849-3800; castlehillinn.com*), right on Ocean Drive in Newport. With the sea crashing just below the clambake pit, you can play bocce or croquet while sipping a cocktail, getting ready for the meal of your life.

Whether on the edge of the Atlantic or far inland, the New England clambake lives on as an expression of American cooking at its most elemental—and delicious.

A traditional clambake at the Chatham Bars Inn in Massachusetts

SPOTLIGHT ON

TOP 15 RHODE ISLAND EVENTS

FEBRUARY

Newport Winter Festival

Come shake off the chill at what's touted as New England's largest winterfest: 10 days of food, music, and fun. Expect kid-pleasing events such as a teddy bear tea, a bounce house, seal-watching tours, and a "princess party." Adults, meanwhile, will appreciate the cocktail contests, ice bar, wine and cheese tastings, and chili cookoff, plus comedy and live music. From beach polo to ice sculpting to an illuminated "garden," the lineup just gets bigger and more diverse, year after year. *401-847-7666; newportwinterfestival.com*

Providence Boat Show

The Ocean State loves its boating, but this show at the Providence Convention Center offers more than pretty watercraft. Attend expert-led seminars on navigation and seamanship; visit with a lineup of special guests; enjoy sea-to-table chef demonstrations; and try your hand at fun, interactive exhibits that put your boat handling and surfing skills to the test. *401-396-9619; providenceboatshow.com*

APRIL-MAY

Daffodil Days at Blithewold Mansion

Spanning thirty-three acres, the Blithewold Mansion Gardens and Arboretum in Bristol is home to one of the most expansive collections of daffodils in the state. Its main attraction, the "Bosquet," shelters 50,000 daffodils in hues of yellow, white, and orange. Come during prime time to see these daffodils in bloom, but don't forget to check out the ten-acre "Great Lawn," the bamboo grove, and historic stonework. *401-253-2707; blithewold.org*

JUNE

Gaspée Days Parade & Weekend

Commemorating the 1772 burning of the British revenue schooner HMS *Gaspée* by American colonists, this Warwick event features one of the most exciting and patriotic parades in the country, complete with colonial fife-and-drum corps, modern-day drum-and-bugle corps, and more. *401-781-1772; gaspee.com*

Newport Flower Show

Nearly 10,000 plant lovers turn up each year for what is arguably—given its setting at the Grand Trianon–style mansion Rosecliff—the classiest flower show in all of New England. While the theme changes from year to year, the three-day extravaganza always kicks off with a not-to-be-missed opening-night party and continues through the weekend with lectures, demonstrations, garden displays, judged horticultural specimens and floral designs, and even children's activities. Separate ticketed events worth checking out include an afternoon tea and a champagne and jazz brunch. *401-847-1000; newportmansions.org*

JULY

South County Hot Air Balloon Festival

The balloons fly and the barbecue sizzles once a year at the University of Rhode Island's athletic fields in Kingston. Enjoy tethered rides or reserve a slot in advance for a free-flying excursion. The sanctioned barbecue championship is sure to see heated competition—and don't miss the beautiful kites taking flight, too. *southcountyballoonfest.com*

Bristol Fourth of July

Bristol might just hold the record for both the longest-running and the longest Fourth of July celebration: The first was held back in 1785, and it has evolved through the years to become a two-week patriotic marathon with a concert series, a beauty pageant, and a carnival. Things really heat up on July 3–4, with a parade, a drum-and-bugle corps competition, and mind-bending fireworks. *fourthofjuly.bristolri.com*

Newport Folk Festival

Since 1959, the Newport Folk Festival has held a unique place in America's musical and cultural history, including as a hub for the Civil Rights movement of the 1960s and as the site of Bob Dylan's famous switch to electric guitar in 1965. Iconic performers like Joan Baez, James Taylor, Joni Mitchell, and Arlo Guthrie got their first major exposure on this Newport stage. Shows sell out well in advance, so plan ahead for next year. *newportfolk.org*

Blessing of the Fleet Weekend

This classic New England event combines a number of attractions. On Friday a ten-mile road race winds its way through scenic Narragansett. It ends up at the Towers, next to Veterans Memorial Park, which is the venue for a major two-day seafood festival that includes live music and fun kids' activities. On Saturday, a colorful parade of watercraft large and small gathers in the Port of Galilee to be blessed by local clergy and vie for prizes. *401-413-9801; narragansettri.com*

AUGUST

Grecian Festival

Founded almost a century ago, this cultural celebration at the Assumption of the Virgin Mary Greek Orthodox Church in Pawtucket features 900 pounds of lamb, 4,000 stuffed grape leaves, and countless Greek pastries. Dancers perform traditional and modern Greek dances, while you enjoy an indoor-outdoor marketplace, a café, and activities for children. *assumptionri.org/GreekFestRI*

Washington County Fair

Held in Richmond, the largest fair in Rhode Island features daily concerts, special acts and events, a giant midway, 4-H shows, and fine arts competitions. This county fair also boasts New England's largest traveling roller coaster, the "battle of the fishermen," and even a goat obstacle course. *401-539-7042; washingtoncountyfair-ri.com*

Rhode Island International Film Festival

Held at locations throughout Newport and Providence, RIIFF showcases independent films with a week of gala celebrations, premieres, VIP guests, industry seminars, educational programs, and award ceremonies, making it the largest film festival in New England. It's also the only one in the region that qualifies films for Academy Award consideration. *401-861-4445; film-festival.org*

Newport Jazz Festival

The granddaddy of jazz festivals takes place in Fort Adams State Park—Rhode Island's beautiful City by the Sea. Enjoy the music of this year's headliners and emerging artists, plus good food and quality craft vendors. *401-848-5055; newportjazz.org*

OCTOBER

Autumnfest

The Blackstone Valley's largest regional fall celebration takes place at Woonsocket's World War II Park and Social Street, and features nonstop live entertainment, food courts, amusement rides, a kids' festival, gigantic fireworks, and a huge Columbus Day parade. *401-526-4278; autumnfest.org*

DECEMBER

Christmas in Newport

The mansions along Newport's Bellevue Avenue sparkle like ornaments on a Christmas tree. In town, simple white lights decorate shop windows, and a month-long calendar of events rings in Christmas in Newport, a tradition that captures the season's essence with historic house tours, outdoor caroling, teas, and *The Nutcracker*. *401-849-6454; christmasinnewport.org*

MASSACHUSETTS
THE BAY STATE

————— ○ —————

From coastal Cape Cod, its beauty sculpted by the Atlantic, to the vibrant arts scene in the western hills, Massachusetts seems to encompass every experience. First, it's a cradle of American history, brimming with Native American heritage, Revolutionary War landmarks, and historic sites like Old Deerfield and Plimoth Plantation, with their fascinating stories waiting to be unwrapped. In Boston, home to Paul Revere and John F. Kennedy, a Navy ship that did battle in the War of 1812 still floats in the harbor.

Massachusetts is also a center of culture, one that radiates outward from the treasure trove of its capital city to encompass seaside towns and rural settings alike. The Berkshires are especially blessed—thanks to the power trio of Tanglewood, Jacob's Pillow, and Mass MoCA—but no matter where you travel in this state, odds are there's a can't-miss arts, shopping, or dining destination nearby.

Finally, Massachusetts might just be the ultimate grab bag of getaways. You can go whale-watching one day and whitewater rafting the next; you can enjoy the solitude of a pristine island beach as well as the energy of a metropolis filled with people from all over the world. Grounded in history but alive with modern adventures, Massachusetts is New England at its most joyfully diverse.

MASSACHUSETTS ESSENTIALS

WESTERN MASSACHUSETTS

BOTANIC GARDEN OF SMITH COLLEGE, NORTHAMPTON

Smith College students live and study inside a botanical showcase. Frederick Law Olmsted's landscape-architecture firm helped lay out the scientific gardens here in the late 19th century, and

there's almost always something in bloom among this collection of more than 6,000 plants. Don't miss the Lyman Conservatory greenhouses, where even in the heart of winter you can sit in a tropical garden and listen to water flowing over the rocks. *413–585–2740; smith.edu/garden*

BRIMFIELD ANTIQUE SHOW, BRIMFIELD

They come seeking old linens, antlers, and vintage marquee lights. City stylists and Brimfield regulars make a beeline for their favorite vendors, while the crowds part whenever Oprah, Martha, Ralph, and their assistants sweep through. But everyone from seasoned pros to the wide-eyed uninitiated stands in awe of the spectacle that is Brimfield. The mother of all antiques markets bursts onto the scene three times a year, in May, July, and September, and each time for six manic days, 6,000 dealers spread over 23 fields, on

(Top) Botanic Garden of Smith College (Bottom) Brimfield Antique Show

a one-mile stretch of Route 20 that cuts through the farm country east of Springfield. A visit to Brimfield can be irresistible and as memorable as a tour through a Middle Eastern bazaar, with the find of a lifetime just over there, at the next booth. *brimfieldshow.com*

CLARK ART INSTITUTE, WILLIAMSTOWN

Unexpectedly audacious in the scope of its collection, the world-class Clark surpasses every expectation of a small-town art museum. We're in Impressionist heaven here, with more then 30 canvases by Renoir alone, along with Degas, Homer, Whistler, and Sargent. You could spend an afternoon just perusing the extensive holdings of decorative arts and medieval works. Enter the original museum through the dramatic new Clark Center and climb the hill behind the building to the Lunder Stone Hill Center for more galleries and a café overlooking the valley. For those who want to combine an active day with art-appreciation, the 140-acre museum grounds are webbed with gorgeous walking trails. *413-458-2303; clarkart.edu*

DID YOU KNOW? Toll House cookies were born when—East Walpole—native, Ruth Wakefield ran out of nuts for her "Butter Drop-Do" cookies. She put a chopped bar of Nestlé's semi-sweet chocolate into the dough instead. As the recipe got around, the folks at Nestlé noticed an increase in sales in the Boston area, figured out the cause, and started scoring their chocolate bars for easier breaking.

(Top and bottom) Clark Art Institute

DEERFIELD RIVER RAFTING

The Deerfield River surges in the Berkshire towns around Charlemont, as power company dam releases cause rapids to tumble down two stretches of the river. You will gasp at the exhilarating Class IV rapids of the Dryway and enjoy the mellower Class II and III rapids farther south, in the deep pools of Zoar Gap. But you don't have to own a kayak to get a taste of this New England whitewater. Zoar Outdoor takes adrenaline junkies down the river in sturdy rafts. *800-532-7483; zoaroutdoor.com*

GUEST HOUSE AT FIELD FARM, WILLIAMSTOWN

An overnight at Field Farm is truly a one-of-a-kind experience. The original house was built for modern art collectors Lawrence and Eleanor Bloedel in 1948, and the influence of the Bauhaus movement remains throughout the rooms, which are filled with modern art and furniture. Lose yourself in the sculpture gardens or feel free to wander farther afield, since the Guest House is in the midst of more than 300 acres of conservation land, with miles of trails and sweeping views of Mount Greylock. *413-458-3135; fieldfarm.org*.

KEYSTONE ARCH BRIDGES TRAIL, CHESTER

In 1841, Western Railroad opened the first rail line to cross Massachusetts from east to west. Its route over the Berkshire highlands was made possible only by the construction of a series of 10 magnificent keystone arch bridges over the Westfield River. Five of the huge relics still stand, and two remain in continued use, now carrying Amtrak passengers and CSX freight. Thanks to the Keystone Arch Bridges Trail, it's possible to visit most of the survivors via a 5-mile round-trip hike through the largest roadless wilderness area in Massachusetts. *413-354-7752; keystonearches.com*

A modern art sculpture on the grounds of Field Farm.

MAIN AND RAILROAD STREETS, GREAT BARRINGTON

At some point in the last few decades of its 250-plus-year history, Great Barrington became Chef Central, and on any given weekend the southern Berkshire town teems with diners—their cars circling like hungry cats, prowling for parking with easy access to restaurants on Main Street and Railroad Street. In a place where there's one restaurant for every 150 residents, the choices are deliciously wide-ranging. Sample a French pastry pick-me-up at Patisserie Lenox and a scoop of velvety "Dirty Chocolate" ice cream at SoCo Creamery. Or dive into full-on farm-to-table dining at Prairie Whale, elegant small plates at Allium, and pro-grade sushi at Bizen. You could go broke working your way through the full menu of eateries here, but it might be worth it. *413-528-4284; southernberkshirechamber.com*

MASS MOCA, NORTH ADAMS

Recent renovations of this bold museum have actually made a collection of old brick mill buildings one of the largest contemporary art museums in the entire world.

Rafting on the Deerfield River

Mass MOCA

View from Mt. Greylock

Norman Rockwell Museum

More than 100 large-scale wall drawings designed by Connecticut native Sol LeWitt are a must-see extravaganza of pattern and color, and changing exhibitions make the rest a new experience every year or so. Leave time to explore the entire dynamic complex, where gigantic gallery spaces let artists unleash their creativity through fascinating installations. *413-662-2111; massmoca.org*

> **DID YOU KNOW?** The Ballpoint pen was patented by John J. Loud of Weymouth, Massachusetts, in 1888.

MOHAWK TRAIL

The fast way to reach the Berkshires from the east is to hop on the Massachusetts Turnpike (I-90) and set your cruise control. Or you can drive through history—slowly, windows open, stopping here and there, taking photos, drinking in the mountain views that have drawn people for nearly a century. The Mohawk Trail is the section of Route 2, from Orange to Williamstown, a delicious 65 miles or so of tourist traps, curves, rises, declines, and one hold-your-breath hairpin turn above the Hoosic Valley that's an attraction in its own right. If this were an amusement park, you'd pay for the chance to experience it, and in fact the first commercial foliage tours did wend their way along this road. They were onto something special, and the Trail rarely lets you down. *866-743-8127; mohawktrail.com*

MOUNT GREYLOCK STATE RESERVATION

At 3,491 feet, Mount Greylock is the highest point in Massachusetts (and a must-see foliage destination), with eye-popping views of the Berkshires and beyond. The reservation offers 70 miles of designated trails for hiking and mountain biking, including an 11½-mile section of the Appalachian National Scenic Trail. At the base of the

mountain, in Lanesborough, you'll find a visitor center where you can pick up a trail map before starting your upward trek. For the less hiking-inclined, Mount Greylock also sports a vista-filled 8-mile auto road to the summit. *413-499-4262; mass.gov*

NORMAN ROCKWELL MUSEUM, STOCKBRIDGE

The great American illustrator Norman Rockwell lived in the Berkshires town of Stockbridge from 1953 until his death in 1978 at age 84. He loved the town, and it loved him back. The Norman Rockwell Museum was founded in 1969 with the help of Rockwell and his wife, Molly. The museum's current home, built in 1993, is set on 36 scenic acres and houses the largest collection of original Norman Rockwell art in the world. There's something special about viewing Rockwell's iconic images of American life in the idyllic little town where many of them were created. Temporary exhibitions also delve into all facets of illustration, from comic books and cartoons to animation. *413-298-4100; nrm.org*

OLD DEERFIELD

Time and Route 5 may have passed the village of Old Deerfield by, but history lovers never do. Along wide mile-long Main Street, a dozen of the immaculately restored and maintained houses are preserved as museums, though at first glance, it's not easy to tell which are museums and which are private homes. Founded in the 1660s and twice sacked in Indian raids, Old Deerfield is preserved from modern encroachment by Historic Deerfield, which runs many of the house

> **DID YOU KNOW?** In 1925, Clarence Birdseye created a new era in the modern grocery industry from his headquarters in Gloucester, Massachusetts, perfecting ways to quick-freeze fish, meat, poultry, fruits, and vegetables.

Old Sturbridge Village

museums. If the number and scope of the houses is a little daunting to you, try the Memorial Hall Museum, which sums up tidily the town's history through photographs, paintings, and historic costumes. *413-774-5581; historic-deerfield.org*

OLD STURBRIDGE VILLAGE, STURBRIDGE

Dramatic events are not the only stuff of history in Old Sturbridge Village. This outdoor museum depicts a rural New England village and does a superb job of capturing the details of daily life from 1790 to 1840. See grain being ground into flour and a blacksmith at work; test your skills at milking a cow, husking corn, or spinning. Heirloom gardens feature fruits, vegetables, herbs, and ornamental flowers. It all makes for a fascinating tapestry—just ask award-winning Ken Burns, who made his first documentary here while still a student at Hampshire College. *800-733-1830; osv.org*

Old Deerfield's first museum house, the Ashley House

Old Sturbridge Village

RED APPLE FARM, PHILLIPSTON

Run by fourth-generation farmer Al Rose, Red Apple Farm offers the full gamut of apple orchard attractions, including a farm stand, weekend barbecues, hay rides, cider donuts and fudge, and farm animals to pet. But Red Apple is no show-farm—it also operates a diverse horticultural program with more than 50 apple varieties, from Arkansas Black to Roxbury Russet. Right by the entrance, you'll find an apple tree that has been grafted with nearly all 50 of the farm's varieties sprouting off a single trunk, a spectacular sight that is worth the trip, and makes Red Apple Farm one of our favorite apple orchards in Massachusetts. *800-628-4851; redapplefarm.com*

RED LION INN, STOCKBRIDGE

While the world is full of verandas and breezeways and front stoops, there's hardly a front porch comparable to that of the Red Lion Inn. Dating back to 1773, the sprawling Main Street structure is known for its authentic historic character, with a working birdcage elevator, converted telephone "booths" off the main

Red Lion Inn

➡ CULTURE IN THE COUNTRY

The Berkshire Hills region of Western Massachusetts has often been described as "America's premier cultural resort," and one visit is all it takes to understand why. As a popular vacation retreat for turn-of-the-century urban elite, it developed a rich arts and entertainment scene that continues to thrive here more than a century later.

There may be no better place to spend a summer evening than at **Tanglewood** (*888-266-1200; bso.org/tanglewood*), the longtime seasonal home of the Boston Symphony Orchestra. Ditch that fancy dress for blue jeans, and dinner reservations for picnic baskets, and stroll the verdant 529-acre campus as the breeze carries the notes of musicians warming up. If the weather's cooperating, the cheapest seats are also the best in the house: on the grass and under the stars. This dreamy combination of artistry, community, and nature has made Tanglewood a favorite destination for more than 350,000 visitors each year, not to mention some of the world's finest performers.

Jacob's Pillow

To quote the Bard himself, "the play's the thing" at **Shakespeare & Company** (*413-637-3353; shakespeare. org*), a dynamic complex with 3 theater spaces, including the tented Rose Footprint that approximates Shakespeare's first London stage. More than 60,000 patrons flock here annually to soak up the performances at one of the largest Shakespeare festivals in the country, operating year-round. Each season's mix of Shakespearean and contemporary drama is distinguished by the company's fierce commitment to the spoken word in all its emotional complexity.

Olympia Dukakis, Paul Giamatti, and Bradley Cooper are just a few of the stars who have made their way to the classic New England campus of Williams College to take part in the Tony-winning **Williamstown Theatre Festival** (*413-458-3253; wtfestival.org*), founded in 1955. From late June to the end of August, it hosts a lineup of classic dramas and new productions on its 2 stages, as well as offering cabaret shows, readings, and workshops.

Much about **Jacob's Pillow** (*413-243-9919; jacobspillow.org*) dance center, school, and theater space has remained unchanged since 1931, when dancer and choreographer Ted Shawn first bought a family farm to create a home for dance. Many of the buildings retain their original architecture; standing proudly in the middle of the campus is the 620-seat Ted Shawn Theatre, built in 1942 from hand-hewn native pine. Far from the highway at "The Pillow," you'll find little to distract from the verdant scenery, birdsong, and, of course, world-class dancing. For 10 weeks every summer, performers from across the globe descend on Lenox to take part in the longest-running international dance festival in America, with stunning views of the Berkshires all around.

lobby, period furnishings, and long list of high-profile guests, including five U.S. presidents. But the wicker-strewn front porch is inarguably its most-photographed claim to fame. An army of rocking chairs stands sentinel behind columns, guaranteeing that no activity on Main Street goes unnoticed or unremarked. To sit and rock at the Red Lion is to understand precisely how longtime resident Norman Rockwell saw Stockbridge. *413-298-5545; redlioninn.com*

DID YOU KNOW? 'Butternut' squash was introduced to the U.S. by Breck Seed Co. of Boston in 1936, having been bred from the Canada Crookneck.

SHELBURNE FALLS

Rivers usually divide towns, but here two bridges across the Deerfield River link the shopping blocks of Buckland and Shelburne to create one unusual village called Shelburne Falls. The gracefully arched stone Bridge of Flowers, built in 1908 to carry trolleys, is planted with hundreds of varieties of flowers and even some trees. It's a splendid walkway that also features a war memorial. The neighboring auto bridge, made of iron, its spidery superstructure painted green, dates back to 1890. Both bridges are reflected in the glassy river, which is impounded just downstream. Walkways overlook the dam, the falls, and a cluster of colorful rocks known as glacial potholes. *413-625- 2544; shelburnefalls.com*

Bridge of Flowers in Shelburne Falls

BOSTON AND SUBURBS

ARNOLD ARBORETUM, BOSTON

From the Orange Line's Forest Hills stop, a clearly-marked 10-minute stroll leads to the visitors' center of the Arnold Arboretum, Harvard University's library of woody plants from around the world that can grow in the New England climate. More than 4,500 kinds of trees, shrubs, and vines are laid out across the rolling 265-acre landscape shaped by Frederick Law Olmsted. But this jewel in the Emerald Necklace is not just green. From the puffy silver pussywillows of March to the incandescent foliage maple groves in October, the arboretum sports a changing coat of pink, red, purple, yellow, gold, and orange. Climb the 240-foot summit of Peters Hill— the second-highest point in Boston—and you'll see the spires of Back Bay and the Financial District in the distance. *617-524-1718; arboretum.harvard.edu*

BOSTON CREAM PIE AT THE PARKER HOUSE, BOSTON

Never was there a more enigmatic piece of pastry than the Boston cream pie. First, it isn't a pie at all—it's cake. And although the Parker House Hotel (now the Omni Parker House) is widely acknowledged as this dessert's birthplace back in in 1856, no one can say for sure how the name came about. What *is* clear is that the Boston cream pie, with its satiny chocolate glaze and custard-filled layers of butter cake, has achieved celebrity status. In 1996, it was named the official state dessert of Massachusetts. Tip your hat to tradition, and order up a slice at the stately hotel restaurant where it got its start. *617-227-8600; omnihotels.com /hotels/boston-parker-house*

BOSTON PUBLIC MARKET, BOSTON

Taste true regional flavor at this indoor food market, which opened at the Haymarket T station in 2015 with the mission of showcasing food and products from the region's six states. Many of the 40-odd vendors offer snacks, drinks, and full meals to go, from the stellar grilled-cheese sandwich at the Cellars at Jasper Hill stand, to the smoked haddock chowder at Boston Smoked Fish Company, to a reuben from Beantown Pastrami Company. Finish it off with ice cream from Crescent Ridge Dairy, fresh cider doughnuts from Red Apple Farm, or a marshmallow confection from Sweet Lydia's. Don't forget to take home some yogurt and cheese from Appleton Farms, or leafy

Boston Public Market

Brattle Book Shop

Boating on the Charles River

greens from Corner Stalk Farm. The only tough part is deciding where to stop. *617-973-4909; bostonpublicmarket.org*

BRATTLE BOOK SHOP, BOSTON

In downtown Boston, Brattle Book Shop, the oldest continuously operating bookstore in America, reminds us about the simple, intimate pleasure of holding a book that once was held by another. Located on a crooked little downtown street, this Dickensian shop is a three-floor wonderland of rare, used, and out-of-print gems. Browse for hours or let second-generation owner Ken Gloss and his devoted staff help you unearth your pleasure. An outdoor sale area showcases best-sellers and curiosities for as little as $1. *617-542-0210; brattlebookshop.com*

CHARLES RIVER PADDLING

For an unforgettable experience, hit the water in a canoe, kayak, or paddleboard from Charles River Canoe & Kayak, with several Boston-area locations including one in the heart of it all, Cambridge's

→ A BRIEF HISTORY OF BOSTON SEAFOOD

An early menu for the Atwood & Bacon Oyster House, which opened in 1826 just up the street from Boston's Faneuil Hall, lists Virginia, Narragansett, and Cape oysters at 15 cents per dozen; fried and stewed scallops for 35 or 30 cents, and a 5 cent apple pie. Being a traditional oyster house, Atwood & Bacon did not serve fish. But it still thrived—Bostonians have always loved their oysters—and later became the **Union Oyster House** (*617-227-2750; unionoysterhouse.com*), now the oldest continuously operated restaurant in the country.

True to its heritage, Union Oyster hews closely to the classics: lobster, chowder, broiled scrod, and seafood Newburg, with the occasional scampi and bouillabaisse. It represents the Old School of Fish, so to speak, the first epoch in Boston's evolution as a seafood town. Another notable member is the century-old **No Name Restaurant** (*617-423-2705; nonamerestaurant.com*), which never got around to naming itself, so why mess with a good thing? Other members include the Italian Old School **Daily Catch** (*617-772-4400; thedailycatch. com*), the upscale **Atlantic Fish Company** (*617-267-4000; atlatnticfishco.com*), and the affordable **Yankee Lobster** (*617-345-9799; yankeelobatercompany.com*).

The Boston seafood landscape shifted in 2003, when Barbara Lynch and Garrett Harker opened the South End's **B&G Oyster** (*617-423-0550; bandgoysters. com*), serving upscale takes on chowder and fried clams, but also *brandade, branzino*, and butter-poached lobster. **Neptune Oyster** (*617-742-3474; neptuneoyster. com*) followed in 2005, and **Ostra**, **Row 34**, and **Island Creek Oyster Bar** cemented the new era of what we'll call the Modern New England School of Fish.

Which brings us to the New School of Fish. With the opening of **Waypoint** (*617-864-2300; waypointharvard.com*), on the outskirts of Cambridge's Harvard Square, Michael Scelfo crossed an invisible line in the sand. No longer obliged to serve chowder or lobster rolls, Scelfo calls his menu "coastally inspired," a bit of wordplay that guarantees Waypoint's freedom from broiled scrod, and begins a deep dive into everything from octopus and uni to crudo and caviar. Along similar lines, Back Bay newcomer **Mooncusser Fish House** (*617-917-5193; mooncusserfishhouse.com*) is cooking farm-and-sea-to-table seasonal fare. At these restaurants, the primary protein may be fish, but the world is their oyster.

Kendall Square. Whether you go solo or join one of the tours, the views of Boston and Cambridge, the Esplanade, and the Zakim Bridge are simply spectacular. If you don't know how, they offer classes. *617-965-5110; paddleboston.com*

CLUB PASSIM, CAMBRIDGE

It's hard to believe that back in 2008 as Club Passim prepared to celebrate it's 50th anniversary, the venue almost collapsed with just $14.00 left in their bank account. But people decided the legendary music venue that had hosted everyone from Joan Baez to Regina Spektor was worth saving. Donors and management stuck with it, Harvard University forgave two months' rent, and the crowds kept coming. Audiences enjoy the intimate concerts; artists love the quiet, attentive crowd that always seems to "get it." The sense of community at the heart of folk music is thick in the room, and that community is the reason the club survives. Today, Passim hosts around 400 concerts a year. *617-492-7679; passim.org*

USS Constitution

DeCordova Museum

DeCORDOVA MUSEUM AND SCULPTURE PARK, LINCOLN

Devoted to discovering and promoting cutting-edge New England artists since 1950, the DeCordova encompasses 30-plus acres of beautifully rolling landscape, including the original house of renowned art collector Julian DeCordova. It's the largest sculpture park in New England, and the lawn furniture, so to speak, is some of the most expressive. Given the large scale of so many pieces of contemporary sculpture, the great outdoors makes an ideal setting. Bring your own picnic or visit the café. *781-259-8355; decordova.org*

FREEDOM TRAIL TOURS, BOSTON

No trip to Boston is complete without a couple of stops on the Freedom Trail, the 2½-mile route past 16 of the city's best-known historical landmarks, including the USS *Constitution*, the Old North Church, and the Bunker Hill Monument. You can certainly navigate the trail on your own, following the red line on the sidewalks. But you'll learn a lot more about Boston's role in the Revolutionary War and the growth of a new nation by taking a free tour led by a knowledgeable and enthusiastic park ranger. Echoes of rifle blasts, secret meetings, and fiery meetinghouse speeches come back to life during the dramatic hour-long Freedom Trail tours, in-depth explorations that will make you question just what was in those baked beans that generated so many firebrands, including William Bainbridge and Joseph Warren. *617-242-5601; nps.gov/bost*

→ UNEXPECTED TREASURES OF THE BOSTON PUBLIC LIBRARY

Just about any destination you head to in Boston takes you past the Boston Public Library on Copley Square. The building itself is a grand bit of architecture and artwork, with structural references to Italian palaces, soaring coffered and vaulted tile ceilings, a central courtyard, a sculpture garden, paintings by John Singer Sargent, and two restaurants in case you need to feed more than your hunger for knowledge. But the real treasures here may be the hundreds of rare manuscripts and arcane artifacts.

Many of these rarities are from far back in history, like two of the earliest printed editions of Dante's *Divine Comedy* and two copies of the first book printed in British North America, the *Bay Psalm Book*, published in Cambridge, Massachusetts, in 1640. An illuminated *Catholicon* of Giovanni Balbi of Genoa is the first dictionary in Western history printed with movable type and one of only 10 copies in the U.S. With more than 700 double-columned vellum pages, it is believed to have been printed by Gutenberg himself in 1460. The oldest artifacts may be 2350 B.C. Babylonian cuneiform tablets that record bills of

sale and receipt for animals delivered for ritual sacrifice.

You can find signed editions, like a manuscript copy of Robert Frost's "Ten Books That Should Be in Every Public Library" and a 1773 copy of *Poems on Various Subjects, Religious and Moral* by Phillis Wheatley, the first published African American poet. You can find beautifully illustrated books, like the complete, hand-colored edition of John James Audubon's *Birds of America* in double elephant folio, or a 33½-foot-long, illuminated 15th-century French manuscript scroll, recording the history of the world from creation to the year 1380. And you can find comprehensive collections, like President John Adams's personal library of 3,500 volumes, or original materials relating to the murder trial and execution of Boston anarchists Sacco and Vanzetti, including their ashes, death masks, and coroner's report.

It's not just reading materials, either. The BPL has the first Congressional Gold Medal, presented to George Washington by the Continental Congress in commemoration of the evacuation of British troops from Boston, the first major victory of the American Revolution. And for those with a more macabre interest, you can gaze at locks of hair from Robert Browning, John Brown, and John Hancock.

Take your time at the BPL. Slow down, explore, read. You just might find a day of enlightenment. *617-536-5400; bpl.org*

FENWAY MUSEUMS, BOSTON

In 1898, when Isabella Stewart Gardner decided to build a Venetian-style palace to house her personal art collection, Fenway was considered part of the wild and wooded outskirts, far from the heart of the city. But Gardner delighted in flouting expectation. After her death, the house and art collection became her namesake museum, and her personality still pervades the place. The Museum of Fine Arts followed Gardner's lead, erecting its own Renaissance palace on Huntington Avenue less than a decade later. Spend an hour, a day, a week—there's no way to see it all. Start with the Impressionists, the Egyptian and Nubian collection, and the American silver, including examples by Paul Revere. Two blocks up Huntington Avenue you can also find the art galleries of the Massachusetts College of Art, the largest free contemporary art space in New England, and learn what today's artists are up to. *617-267-9300, mfa.org; 617-566-1401, gardnermuseum.org; 617-879-7000 massart.edu*

FENWAY PARK, BOSTON

The oldest active Major League field and widely considered the most famous ballpark in America, Fenway has earned the right to be quirky. The "Green Monster" 37-foot wall in left field is an artifact of the design constraints of the 1912 lot, as is the short right-field foul line that ends at Pesky's Pole. To appreciate this shrine to America's national pastime, take a tour of this century-old masterpiece, walk the field and touch the Green Monster, and look down on the diamond from the press box. *617-226-6666; boston.redsox.mlb.com*

HARVARD UNIVERSITY, CAMBRIDGE

Since the founding of Harvard College in 1636 some of the brightest scholars in the world have strolled through its green yard. Grabbing a selfie in front of the statue of founder John Harvard has become as much of a tourist draw here as the swan boats are in the Boston Public Garden. Among the other highlights is the Widener Library, third largest in the country, which holds over 3 million volumes. Across from Harvard Yard is the world-class Harvard Art Museum, while just a few blocks north is the equally worthy Peabody Museum of Archeology and the Harvard Museum of Natural History, home to a one-of-a-kind collection of handblown glass flowers. The buildings of Harvard University speak of history and a bit of mystery. Take a listen. *harvard.edu/on-campus/visit-harvard/tours*

DID YOU KNOW? In 1834 Daniel Chapin sold the first friction matches door to door in Chicopee, Massachusetts.

The Edward M. Kennedy Institute for the U.S. Senate was dedicated in 2015

KENNEDY MUSEUMS, BOSTON

Housed in an I.M. Pei-designed tower rising from the Boston waterfront, the John F. Kennedy Library and Museum dwells on the aspirations and hopes of a country during the brief term of its 35th president. The period settings and multimedia exhibits re-create the excitement and tensions of the Kennedy years, from John and his brother Robert conferring in the Oval Office during the Cuban Missile Crisis to the president's rousing challenge to the nation to put a man on the moon. Next door is the newer Edward M. Kennedy Institute for the U.S. Senate, where visitors can explore the younger Kennedy's Senate legacy and try their hand at being legislators in a reproduction of the U.S. Senate chambers. Together these museums commemorate a family who gave their lives to public service, and more importantly celebrate the promise and hope of American government. *617-514-1600, jfklibrary. org; 617–740–7000, emkinstitute.org*

THE MAPPARIUM, BOSTON

The Mary Baker Eddy Library is home to a one-of-a-kind structure: the world's only walk-in, stained-glass globe that allows the surface of the earth to be viewed without distortion. Three stories high and measuring 30 feet in diameter, this illuminated exhibit is composed of 206 LED fixtures, which when programmed together produce at least 16 million colors. The Mapparium also features what's known as a "whispering gallery" because of its unique acoustics. Someone speaking quietly at one end of the Mapparium can be heard with perfect clarity by someone at the opposite end. Inside the Mapparium, every visitor's voice can be heard—symbolizing, in a way, how we are all truly global citizens. *617-450-7000; marybakereddylibrary.org*

DID YOU KNOW? The paper bag was patented by Luther C. Crowell from West Dennis, Massachusetts, in 1872.

(Above) The Mapparium (Left) Minute Man National Historical Park.

MINUTE MAN NATIONAL HISTORICAL PARK, CONCORD AND LEXINGTON

The history of the American Revolution comes alive on the 5-mile Battle Road Interpretive Trail between Concord and Lexington, thanks to educational plaques that spark the imagination. Highlights include the North Bridge, where the famous "shot heard 'round the world" was fired on April 19, 1775, and the park headquarters at Buttrick House, whose displays and exhibits include the Hancock Cannon, a piece of artillery that the British were looking for when they marched into Concord. *978-369-6993; nps.gov/mima*

TRAVEL TIP: Two hundred and ninety-four steps doesn't sound like that many at the bottom, but you feel it about halfway up the narrow spire of the Bunker Hill Monument. The view of Boston is worth the trouble.

MOUNT AUBURN CEMETERY, CAMBRIDGE

Waking up early to visit a cemetery might sound like a macabre undertaking, but this is no ordinary cemetery. It was created on the outskirts of Boston in 1831 as America's first rural or garden cemetery, a precursor to parks in urban areas. Today, more than 200,000 annual visitors come to visit the final resting place of a long list of luminaries in American arts and letters, like Henry Wadsworth Longfellow, Winslow Homer, and Buckminster Fuller. Yet others simply follow in the footsteps of Roger Tory Peterson, the renowned ornithologist who once led bird-watching walking tours here. Bring your binoculars,

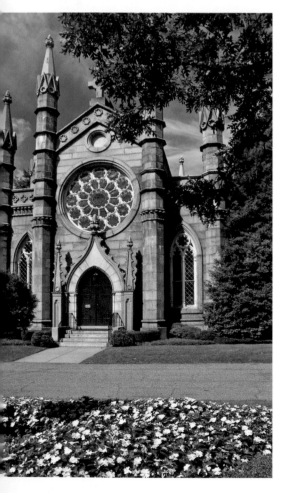

and a naturalist from Massachusetts Audubon will help you spot, say, the scruffy yellow chin of the Northern Parula Warbler. *617-547-7105; mountauburn.org*

MUSEUM OF AFRICAN AMERICAN HISTORY, BOSTON

Boston's road to the abolition of slavery wasn't a straight one, so it's fitting that tours along the Black Heritage Trail aren't either. Examining all the nooks and crannies you'd never have seen on your own, this rambling exploration passes by old stops on the Underground Railroad and the homes of famous abolitionists and ends at the African Meeting House, a gathering place for such legendary anti-slavery activists as Frederick Douglass and William Lloyd Garrison. *617-725-0022, x330; afroammuseum.org*

TEA PARTY SHIPS AND MUSEUM, BOSTON

The image of rabble-rousing patriots dressing up in Indian garb and tossing British tea into the harbor to protest the king's tax policies continues to resonate nearly 250 years later. A lightning bolt in 2001 and a fire in 2007 destroyed the old ship and museum devoted to this singular event in U.S. history, but a new museum and 3 replica ships opened in 2012 to put the Tea Party literally on the map again. Each December the museum, in collaboration with the Old South Meeting House, hosts a lively reenactment of the Boston Tea Party that we highly recommend. *866-955-0667; bostonteapartyship.com*

(Left) Located within picturesque Mount Auburn Cemetery is the Gothic Revival style Bigelow Chapel.

DID YOU KNOW? George F. Grant was Harvard's first African American professor, and in his spare time invented the wooden golf tee.

(This page) Scenes from the Tea Party Ships and Museum

WALDEN POND STATE RESERVATION, CONCORD AND LINCOLN

People from across the world are drawn to this beautiful and peaceful spot where Henry David Thoreau began writing *Walden*. Visit a replica of his one-room cabin, walk the lakeside trail to see where the original 1845 cabin once stood, or hike the trails through 335 acres of protected open space. You can picnic on the beach or, better yet, go for a swim in Walden Pond. Its oasis of clear water, more than 100-feet deep, is a little more crowded than in Thoreau's day, but maybe you'll find your purpose here, too. *978-369-3254; mass.gov*

WORCESTER ART MUSEUM, WORCESTER

This historic stone edifice contains one of New England's finest art and antiquities collections. You will find pre-Columbian New World artifacts, the nation's largest collection of Roman mosaics, and a 12th-century Benedictine chapter house, the first medieval structure to be transported from Europe to America. Whet your appetite amid the glistening fruits of Flemish still lifes in the European galleries, admire the bright palettes of the French Impressionists, and appreciate the equal time given to women artists in the 20th-century American gallery. Take a break in the café, with its garden courtyard, before heading back into this paradise of art. *508-799-4406; worcesterart.org*

> **TRAVEL TIP:** If you're in Wellfleet on Cape Cod in October, stop by their oyster festival for local cuisine, arts and crafts, educational programs, cooking demonstrations, kids' activities, walking tours, live music, a road race, and the oyster shuck-off competition. *wellfleetoysterfest.org*

NORTH & SOUTH SHORES

APPLETON FARMS, IPSWICH

Appleton Farms dates back to 1636, making it one of the nation's oldest continuously operating agricultural enterprises. This nearly 1,000-acre property is now conserved for the public by The Trustees of Reservations, who run interpretive programs highlighting the operations of a working farm. Guides take you through the dairy barn, sheep shed, and draft horse stable to the Great Pasture, where the Ayrshire and Jersey dairy cows graze. Walkers can also enjoy the 5 miles of bridle paths created in the early 1900s, and loop gently through mature woodlands. Don't miss the panoramic vista from Pigeon Hill, with fields rimmed by stone walls rolling down to tree-lined wetland meadows. *978-356-5728; thetrustees.org*

BATTLESHIP COVE, FALL RIVER

Of all the many maritime-themed museums in New England, few immerse the visitor into the sensory world of being aboard ships the way that Battleship Cove does. The ships docked on Fall River's Mount Hope make up the largest collection of preserved U.S. Navy ships in the world, and once were home to hundreds of sailors, many of whom served during wartime. Walk through the cavernous spaces of the USS *Massachusetts*, and it's not difficult to imagine the sounds of the furious fighting the ship experienced during World War II. Explore the tight corners of a submarine, the guns of a naval destroyer, and 2 PT boats similar to the one that a young Lieutenant John F. Kennedy once helmed. Ship models, galleries, and films all complete a full day in the presence of these massive ships, built for

war in the never-ending hope they could bring peace. *508-678-1100; battleship-cove.org*

CLAM SHACKS, ESSEX

The Essex River Basin is known for having the sweetest clams in New England, and if you drive into town after a day at the beach, you'll no doubt find a line out the door at seafood specialist Woodman's. Join the queue and you'll soon smell the fryer; it's here that the first fried clam is said to have been invented over a century

➡ INDIAN PUDDING

Few New England desserts can compete with the historical pedigree of a bowl of warm, spicy Indian pudding. The dish got its start when early colonists brought with them to America a fondness for "hasty pudding"—an English dish made by boiling wheat flour and water until it thickens into porridge. Without wheat, the homesick settlers adapted by using native cornmeal, known as "Indian flour," and changed the name of the dish to reflect its new main ingredient. Later, milk from New England's flourishing dairy industry replaced water, and spices and molasses were added. The result, baked in a slow oven for hours, was a cold-weather classic, born of homesickness and fed by what was available and affordable, resulting in a unique combination of New England flavors.

Today, we still look forward to steaming bowls of wobbly, fragrant, perfectly golden-brown pudding, served either plain or topped with a scoop of vanilla ice cream, creating a bonus slurp-worthy sauce as it melts. Rich in colonial history as Massachusetts is, it's no surprise the state has a number of restaurants turning out deliciously authentic versions of this dish. The newest of these is Springfield's **Student Prince** (*413-734-7475; studentprince.com*), which started serving the pudding in 1935. The other three are all much older, including Boston's **Durgin-Park** (*617-227-2038; arkrestaurants.com/durgin_park*), located in the 17th-century marketplace of Faneuil Hall. Out in Sudbury you can enjoy this dish at **Longfellow's Wayside Inn** (*978-443-1776; wayside.org*), or in Concord at **Concord's Colonial Inn** (*978-369-9200; concordscolonialinn.com*). Both date from 1716, and as you eat a bowl of warm pudding and ice cream, your taste buds will travel back in time.

Crane Beach

ago. An alternative to Woodman's is J.T. Farnham's, a cozy seafood shack with views of the Essex River and sweet and briny clams harvested fresh from the cold Ipswich waters. Here, though, the clams are dipped in an egg wash and cornmeal before getting their hot oil bath, whereas at Woodman's they're coated with milk and corn flour. Either choice will make you re-evaluate your relationship to bivalves. *800-649-1773, woodmans.com; 978-768-6643, jtfarnhams.com*

COGSWELL'S GRANT, ESSEX

Set on 165 acres overlooking the Essex River, the 1728 farmhouse at Cogswell's Grant would be reason enough to visit, but it's even more engrossing to see how pioneering folk-art collectors Bertram K. and Nina Fletcher Little furnished their summer home. From birdhouses to carved ostrich and emu eggs, whirligigs to Shaker boxes, faux-painted furniture to fruit-themed pincushions, you'll find abundant

DID YOU KNOW? Launched in 1797 in Boston, the USS *Constitution* is the world's oldest commissioned warship still afloat.

proof of the inventiveness and creativity of early American craftspeople. *978-768-3632; historicnewengland.org*

CRANE BEACH, IPSWICH

For sheer scenic beauty, no New England strand tops Crane Beach, another jewel in the treasure chest of properties owned by the nonprofit Trustees of Reservations. This four-mile stretch of soft, white sand is set against a backdrop of undulating dunes, piping plovers, and the grand mansion at Castle Hill. If you walk a bit, you'll find a private spot, even in high summer. There are also plenty of shallows and tidepools for kids to explore. Locals caution that July's greenhead flies can be pesky—but the months before and after are heaven. *978-356-4351; thetrustees.org*

DOGTOWN, ROCKPORT AND GLOUCESTER

Searching through her grandfather's attic, local graphic designer Seania McCarthy discovered a clipping about a deserted village in the heart of Cape Ann called Dogtown Common. A prosperous farming and mill community in the 1600s and 1700s, it was finally abandoned, literally, to the dogs in the mid-19th century. Now she gives hiking

Cogswell's Grant

GLOUCESTER MARITIME HERITAGE CENTER, GLOUCESTER

Gloucester is one of the few places in New England that still depends on the sea for its industrial livelihood, and nowhere is that legacy of boatbuilding, ship repair, commercial fishing, and salvage diving more accessible than at the Gloucester Maritime Heritage Center. The former shipyard's main feature is a marine railway in operation since 1849, and is often hauling some antique wooden vessel out for restoration. Boatbuilding is on view in the dory shop and boathouse, where classes are taught on constructing personal rowing and sailing craft. In the Sea Pocket Lab, kids will enjoy various touch tanks of marine critters that you'd find around the harbor's piers or offshore in the Gulf of Maine. *978-281-0470; maritime.gloucester.org*

tours of the area, complete with tales of former villagers. Hidden among the trees, in addition to old cellar holes, are huge boulders carved with quirky inspirational messages such as "Never Try Never Win" that were commissioned by a philanthropist during the Depression. *978-546-8122; walkthewords.com*

TRAVEL TIP: Nantucket's annual celebration of all things daffodil includes art shows, tours, an antique car parade, tailgate picnic, window decorating contest, and the annual Nantucket Daffodil Flower Show. *daffodilfestival.com*

Gloucester Fisherman's Memorial

CRANBERRY BOGS

It's not often that a farmer's hard work brings tour buses filled with camera-toting visitors, or families with children, or those who yearn for autumn beauty. But when New England's cranberry farmers bring in their crops each fall, they know they'll have company.

Cranberry bogs are composed of sand and peat, and on their own they wouldn't interest most people. When the berries ripen on the vines, however, and farmers begin "wet harvesting"—flooding the bogs with water until they become a sea of crimson—the grand show of color begins.

In Massachusetts, cranberries have long reigned as the top food crop. In fact, the state is home to the world's largest cranberry processor, grower-owned cooperative Ocean Spray Cranberries. The southeastern part of the state is the hot spot for "cranberry peeping," and if you head west from Plymouth down Seven Hills Road and out Federal Furnace Road, you'll see plenty. You can also try along Routes 106 and 44, or south on 58, through Carver, Wareham, and Middleborough, and through Kingston, Plympton, and Halifax. Wherever the eye looks, it's a sight to remember.

A number of farmers welcome visitors, and some even let you close to the bogs (*cranberries. org/visit*). Many will pause in their work—as generations before them have—to talk bogs and berries. On Columbus Day weekend at the **Cranberry Harvest Celebration** (*508-322-4000; facebook. com/cranberryharvest*) in Wareham, you can see all phases of the traditional dry harvest for fresh fruit or the colorful wet harvest with fruit destined for juice, sauce, and so on. Learn how cranberries are incorporated into cooking and crafts, and enjoy live music, a farmers' market, and more.

A different sort of experience is yours at the **Edaville Railroad** (*508-866-8190; edaville.com*) in South Carver. Part of the Edaville Family Theme Park, this historic narrow-gauge railway takes park visitors on a 20-minute ride through a 1,300-acre cranberry plantation. Meanwhile, in Middleborough **On Cranberry Pond** (*508-946-0768; oncranberry pond.com*) lets you wake up right in the heart of cranberry country at a peaceful 6-room bed-and-breakfast surrounded by a working bog.

ISLAND CREEK OYSTERS, DUXBURY

No ingredient expresses its provenance like an oyster. Oysters' flavor and texture are influenced heavily by the place they come from, and Duxbury, it turns out, is a great place to live if you're an oyster. These are the oysters you get at Per Se in New York and any raw bar worth its salt. You can explore the source by booking a tour at the Island Creek Oysters farming co-op, where the folks will show you around their operation on beautiful Duxbury Bay and serve up samples of the delectable harvest. A more flexible but equally tasty option is to visit one of the co-op's namesake oyster bars in Boston and Burlington. *781-934-2028; islandcreekoysters.co*

THE LANTERN ROOM, NEWBURYPORT

Lighthouses are inherently romantic. But toss in dinner for two, and you have an evening that would make Casanova weak in the knees. Reservations are available from April through December at the Lantern Room of the Newburyport Rear Range Light Tower, which overlooks Newburyport Harbor in Massachusetts. Diners have a choice of menus from five local restaurants, but the food really takes a backseat to the gorgeous lighthouse. *800-727-2326; lighthousepreservation.org*

NEW BEDFORD WHALING MUSEUM, NEW BEDFORD

There's nothing like a 66-foot whale skeleton to get you jazzed to learn more about New Bedford, the 19th-century whaling capital of the country. Or, if you're interested in mammals more your own size, the museum offers invaluable information about the lives of the town's famed inhabitants, including Frederick Douglass and Herman Melville. The museum also runs a film series, a lecture series, and a *Moby-Dick* marathon. *508-997-0046; whalingmuseum.org*

Plimoth Plantation

PLIMOTH PLANTATION, PLYMOUTH

Upward of a million visitors flood into Plymouth every year to experience first-hand what life was like in one of America's first colonies, and for good reason. Plimoth Plantation provides an immersive, 360-degree view of history thanks the its re-creation of a 17th-century English village filled with actors and the Wampanoag Homesite, populated not by actors but by real Native Americans. It also boasts a full-scale reproduction of the *Mayflower II*, although this floating museum is undergoing repairs at Connecticut's Mystic Seaport until at least 2019, in preparation for the blowout celebration the following year to mark the Pilgrims' landing in the New World. *508-746-1622; plimoth.org*

> **DID YOU KNOW?** In 1866 in Springfield, Milton Bradley introduced *The Checkered Game of Life* to board game enthusiasts everywhere.

Oyster farming on Duxbury Bay

New Bedford Whaling Museum

WHALE-WATCHING

One of the best places in the world to spy a whale lies just off the Massachusetts coast, at the Stellwagen Bank National Marine Sanctuary. This 842-square-mile swath of ocean located at the mouth of Massachusetts Bay between Cape Cod and Cape Ann, is a massive nutrient-rich mesa that offers a smorgasbord for humpbacks, finbacks, and minkes. These gentle giants head to Stellwagen Bank from April through November to take huge gulps of fish, and in the process create a whale-watching scene so reliable that local tour companies claim a sighting record of 99 percent.

Cape Ann can rightly be called the state's whale-watching capital, with three venerable family-owned tour companies in Gloucester dedicated to whale expeditions. This small port city is ideally situated at the tip of the cape, between two major feeding grounds—Stellwagen Bank and, to the north, Jeffreys Ledge—which means boats from Gloucester don't have to travel as far to reach whales and dolphins and can instead spend more time among them. Choose from **Seven Seas Whale Watch**, a 2012 *Yankee* Best of New England winner (*978-283-1776; 7seaswhalewatch.com*); **Cape Ann Whale Watch**, which boasts the largest and fastest whale-watch vessel north of Boston (*800-877-5110; seethewhales.com*); and **Capt. Bill & Sons**, which partners with the Whale Center of New England (*978-283-6995; captbillandsons.com*).

Boston's **New England Aquarium Whale Watch** (*877-733-9425; neaq.org, bostonharborcruises.com*) is another popular option. After checking out the aquarium's whale skeleton and nearby life-size replica of a whale's heart, you can head out to see the real deal. The aquarium partners with Boston Harbor Cruises for the trip from Boston Harbor to Stellwagen Bank, and also trains the naturalists who come along for the ride.

If you find yourself north of Gloucester or south of Boston, you can still hop a ride to the whale's playground. Sitting just below the New Hampshire border, **Newburyport Whale Watch** has been leading excursions into the Gulf of Maine for more than half a century (*800-848-1111; newburyportwhalewatch.com*). Down in Plymouth, tour companies include **Plymouth Whale Watching**, based on the same pier as the *Mayflower II* (*508-747-3434; plymouthwhalewatching.com*); while out on Cape Cod, whale-watch boats depart from Nantucket, Hyannis, and especially Provincetown, home to **Dolphin Fleet Whale Watches**, which runs 4 tour boats and lays claim to starting East Coast whale watching decades ago (*800-826-9300; whalewatch.com*).

SALEM

Best known as the site of the Salem witch trials in the 1690s, this seaside city flourished in the 17th and 18th centuries as its merchant vessels circled the globe in ships like the three-masted *Friendship*. A magnificent replica of this ship now bobs alongside the 9-acre Salem Maritime National Historic Site. Captains built homes on the waterfront, including the so-called House of the Seven Gables that Nathaniel Hawthorne made famous in his 1851 novel of the same name. Nearby, the renowned Peabody Essex Museum is the oldest continuously operating museum in the U.S., founded in 1799, and one of the biggest on the East Coast. It stores many of the treasures and artifacts those ships brought back from afar. *877-725-3662; salem.org*

DID YOU KNOW? Every April 19 in Lexington, before the sun has cracked the morning sky, the American Revolution begins, or at least the re-enactment of it.

(Above) The House of the Seven Gables, Salem (Below) Hamilton Hall (named for the founding father) was once a social space for Salem's leading families.

WORLD'S END, HINGHAM

A property of Massachusetts's Trustees of Reservations, World's End is the unusual name of a completely undeveloped peninsula of land that juts out into Hingham Harbor on Massachusetts Bay. The 4 rounded hills that give the place its character are called drumlins, and from their grassy summits there are unexpected views of the Boston skyline 15 miles in the distance. The 251-acre scenic reservation is open to the public for nature study, walking, horseback riding, picnicking, and cross-country skiing. *781-740-7233; thetrustees.org*

DID YOU KNOW? Thanks to the invention of the monkey wrench by Loring Coes of Worcester, today's workmen have only one tool to misplace.

THE CAPE & ISLANDS

AQUINNAH PUBLIC BEACH, MARTHA'S VINEYARD

Hands-down one of the most scenic public beaches in New England is set in the wild southwestern corner of Martha's Vineyard, tucked southeast of the Aquinnah Cliffs. Layers of clay form the cliffs, with varying degrees of vivid color depending on the sedimentary deposit. The result is a dramatic 150-foot backdrop of reds, greens, yellows, and whites, which becomes even more striking at sunset. A 10-minute walk from the parking lot at Aquinnah Lighthouse will bring you to the public portion of the beach. *aquinnah-ma.gov*

Aquinnah Cliffs

Gay Head Lighthouse over Aquinnah

ART'S DUNE TOURS, PROVINCETOWN

You must be doing something right if you're still in business since 1946. Spend an hour in an air-conditioned Suburban as you drive over the sand dunes on Provincetown's Cape Cod National Seashore learning about the unique topography as well as the long-standing dune houses that still cling precariously to the shoreline. Among the newer offerings is a 3½-hour "Land n' Lake" tour that mixes the dune drive with a paddle on saltwater out of East Harbor. Lunch is served on a lake atop a raft. *800-894-1951; artsdunetours.org*

Maple-bacon donut at Back Door Donuts

BACK DOOR DONUTS, MARTHA'S VINEYARD

If you follow a delicious bakery aroma to a long line of people on a warm summer night in Oak Bluffs, you'll likely find yourself at Back Door Donuts. Martha's Vineyard Gourmet Café and Bakery is open regular hours from mid-April to mid-October, but its "back door" opens from 7 p.m. to 1 a.m. The pastries are made fresh on-site in classic flavor options as well as more adventurous ones like maple bacon or butternut crunch. And while you're at it, pick up a few of the perfectly fried, equally sinful apple fritters. *508-693-3688; mvbakery.co*

BIKING NANTUCKET

At 3½ by 14 miles, Nantucket flirts with being too big for an island—it takes a minor amount of mental processing to grasp it all at once. But the place is undeniably possessed of a powerful sense of islandness that neither size nor summer hordes can quell. The best way to dive in

Art's Dune Tours

is by bike, thanks to the flat terrain and handy network of paved bicycle paths. You can bring your own bike over by boat (there's a small charge) or simply rent one from a local outfitter. Outside Nantucket Town, the island has a welcome openness of space, with cranberry bogs and pristine sandy beaches and views seemingly to Portugal. *nantucket.net/activities/biking*

CAPE COD BASEBALL LEAGUE

The promotional tagline for the league—"the stars of tomorrow shine tonight"—couldn't be more accurate. In fact, one in seven major-league baseball players once rounded the bases for the CCBL. These include Red Sox alums Mark Bellhorn (Cotuit '93), Kevin Millar (Harwich '92), Doug Mirabelli (Hyannis '90), Bill Mueller (Bourne '92), and Jason Varitek (Hyannis '91-'93). There's nothing quite like sitting on the third-base line of a field of dreams on a warm summer night, batting away mosquitoes, and eating Cracker Jacks. Games are played around the Cape at various high school fields from mid-June to mid-August, so find yourself a seat in the stands, and watch the stars. *508-432-6909; capecodbaseball.org*

CAPE COD RAIL TRAIL

It wasn't so long ago that this flat, 22-mile-long dedicated bike trail was almost seen as a hazard by the state. Now it's practically a natural resource, with millions of dollars poured into it to rehab bridges, tunnels, and culverts, and to widen and repave the route. The trail, which starts mid-Cape at Route 134 in Dennis and extends to Wellfleet, follows the former Old Colony Railroad bed, past lakes and marshland, forests and harbors. At the Salt Pond Visitor Center in Eastham, don't miss the spur trail heading to the crashing waves of the Atlantic Ocean. Don't have your own wheels? Outfitters along the route are happy to rent you a ride. *mass.gov; capecodchamber.org*

CAPE PLAYHOUSE, DENNIS

Regular visitors to the Cape probably know that Bette Davis got her start at the Cape Playhouse as an usher, and that America's oldest continually operating professional summer theater still leads the Cape's seasonal venues. But fewer may know that it's also home to the Cape Cod Center for the Arts, which sponsors a terrific Children's Theater that introduces youngsters to the art and enchantment of the live stage with inspirational productions. World-class actors from Humphrey Bogart to Betty White, Julie Andrews to Fred Savage, have all graced this stage. Come to the Cape Playhouse to see the next star born. *877-385-3911; capeplayhouse.com*

CAPE POGE WILDLIFE REFUGE NATURAL HISTORY TOUR, MARTHA'S VINEYARD

When you want to get away from the crowds and access the Vineyard's most remote reaches, take an open-vehicle, four-wheel-drive tour of this Chappaquiddick Island refuge. Personable, passionate, and knowledgeable drivers point out unusual plants and birds all along the solitary, sandy shores. And with a maximum of 12 people per trip, there's plenty of space to ask questions. Combine it with a tour of the remote Cape Poge Lighthouse, meander around the quiet Mytoi Gardens, or rent a kayak at Dike Bridge to make a splendid day of it. *508-693-7662; thetrustees.org*

COMMERCIAL STREET, PROVINCETOWN

Provincetown is one of the best people-watching towns in New England. And where those people gather is Commercial Street, the narrow, 3-mile, one-way east-west corridor of cars crawling past throngs of walkers, bicyclists, bikers, and everyone else, happily standing or sitting around at cafés. Jutting out into the sea at the heart of the street is Macmillan Pier, where whale-watching boats depart for the feeding grounds of hundreds of humpbacks. Along the street you will find art galleries, snug cottages, restaurants, bakeries, and shops of every description, and more than a few that defy description. At its western tip the street ends at a breakwater and memorial park, a great spot to sit down and wait for sunset. Afterward, rest up at your inn, have dinner, then return to the street at dark, when the curtain reopens on the galaxy of strollers, the best theater on Cape Cod.

EDWARD GOREY HOUSE, YARMOUTH PORT

Much as artist and author Edward Gorey loved the macabre, his pen-and-ink drawings of all matters horrific were always touched by whimsy, including the animated tombstone opening credits for the

Biking on Cape Cod

Bikes lined up along Edgartown Harbor

CAPE COD NATIONAL SEASHORE

More than 50 years after Cape Cod National Seashore was created, its legacy is still being written. The greatest strength of this sprawling national park is that it is many things: an expansive beach; an empty plain of sand; a bike path; a trek through an oceanside forest; a lighthouse tour; an old military site. Born in an age when coastal terrain was usually turned over for development, this 44,600-acre park preserved the Outer Cape without locking it away. Instead, it has ensured the Cape's survival by providing an up-close opportunity for anyone to find its beauty and wonder.

The Outer Cape has always been "a grand place to be alone and undisturbed," as playwright Eugene O'Neill described it in 1919. He wrote two of his most famous works, *Anna Christie* and *The Hairy Ape* during his own sojourn in the Province Lands. Other artists and writers soon followed and never stopped, from "poet of the dunes" Harry Kemp to more famous visitors like E.E. Cummings, Jack Kerouac, Mary Oliver, Jackson Pollock, and Willem de Kooning. Perhaps most important was Henry Beston, whose 1928 book, *The Outermost House*, brought attention to the sheer wild beauty among the sweeping dunes.

The Seashore's 40-mile coastline encourages endless walking, sunbathing, and swimming. **Coast Guard Beach** marks the beginning of what Henry David Thoreau called "the Great Beach." Historians believe that this is where the crew of the *Mayflower* first spied land in 1620. The beach is wide, with sand dunes, marshland, and pounding waves. No parking in summer, but free transportation is provided via a shuttle bus at the Little Creek parking area in Eastham.

Nauset Light Beach and **Marconi Beach** have the biggest waves, great for surfing or boogie boarding. Plus, Marconi has an observation platform that provides a terrific overview of the Outer Cape, including both ocean and bay. **Head of the Meadow Beach** is often less crowded, and it can also be a prime place to spot some seals. A few years ago a sandbar near this beach attracted hundreds of the playful critters. **Herring Cove Beach** and **Race Point Beach** are considered among the finest on the East Coast. Race Point Beach, on the Cape's outermost point, can sometimes have a strong undertow and is best for experienced swimmers. Herring Cove Beach faces the bay, with its calmer waves. All 6 swimming beaches have showers, restrooms, changing rooms, and lifeguards in summer.

The National Seashore is also dotted with "kettle ponds," which formed when the ice sheets retreated around 18,000 years ago. They're ideal for children and are usually around 10 degrees warmer than the ocean. Most are operated as town swimming beaches. **Great Pond**, **Gull Pond**, and **Long Pond** are the more popular bodies of water, set right off main roads. Visitors can also rent canoes, kayaks, or stand-up paddleboards to use here.

For those who like a more land-locked activity, 3 bike trails wind through the National Seashore. **Province Lands Bike Trail** is a paved 5½-mile scenic loop with views of open dunes, forest, and beach, while **Nauset Bike Trail**'s 1.6-mile stretch ends at Coast Guard Beach and is peppered with views of salt marshes and forest. **Head of the Meadow Trail** is a 2-mile unpaved route that takes riders on a bumpier jaunt to Head of the Meadow Beach.

There are also 12 self-guided hiking trails through the National Seashore, ranging from 15-minute strolls to hour-plus walks, with one 3- to 5-hour hike for the most

ambitious. **Buttonbush Trail** in Eastham is a 15-minute rope-guided hike that winds through forest and crosses over Buttonbush Pond, great for kids. The **Nauset Marsh Trail** loop takes about an hour and winds along the edge of salt-water ponds and Nauset Marsh. The 30-minute **Pilgrim Spring Trail** leads to a site representative of where Pilgrims are thought to have drunk their first fresh water in New England.

Park rangers lead programs through the National Seashore's two visitors' centers, **Salt Pond** in Eastham (*508-255-3421*) and **Province Lands** in Provincetown (*508-487-1256*). Learn the basics of saltwater fishing, explore the tidal flats of Coast Guard Beach, take a canoeing lesson, do yoga on the beach, or join the rangers for a 2- to 4-hour cardiovascular-workout hike. You can go snorkeling or bird-watching, sit around a campfire on the beach, or take part in a scavenger hunt.

Cape Cod National Seashore is a wonderful illustration of democracy. This isn't a gated property, and you don't need a trust fund to get access to it. It's there for all of us—which is what its creators had in mind. *nps.gov/caco*

PBS *Mystery!* series. The house preserves the artist's mishmash collection of books, artifacts, beach stones, and curios—along with his enduring, hilariously droll vision. *508-362-3909; edwardgoreyhouse.org*

GREEN BRIAR NATURE CENTER & JAM KITCHEN, SANDWICH

In 1903, Ida Putnam began selling her jams and jellies to travelers on Route 6A, "the only highway that went all the way to the end of the Cape." Preserves are still cooked in Ida's kettles over the original burners, and you can sample as many as you'd like before buying. Also on site are the interpreted trails and spectacular wildflower garden of the Nature Center, offering programs for kids and adults year-round. Next door you'll find the Briar Patch Conservation Area, the inspiration for the quirky animal characters of Thornton Burgess's beloved children's stories. *508-888-6870; thorntonburgess.org*

MURRAY'S TOGGERY SHOP, NANTUCKET

Gray often seems to be the color of Nantucket, of its Quaker-shingle houses and its island fog. But Nantucket Red, which fades to pink with time, is the color that will represent your love for this island. Philip C. Murray introduced the hue via brick-red sailcloth pants in the 1950s, when he took over his father's clothing shop at the top of the cobblestone Main Street. His color soon became as insider shorthand for the well-heeled but casual Nantucket summer life, and Murray's Toggery remains the only company that can sell official "Nantucket Reds," which it does now in everything from skirts to shirts to pants. *508-228-0437; nantucketreds.com*

NANTUCKET PHARMACY, NANTUCKET

No, you haven't stepped back in time—it just feels that way. The Nantucket Pharmacy, located smack-dab downtown, still features its original 1929 soda fountain counter. Open until 10:30 p.m. during summer to welcome late-night strollers, this place is like something out of a movie set: long counter, black vinyl-topped stools, and a chalkboard menu chock-full of delightful options like peanut-butter-and-jelly sandwiches and coffee frappes. *508-228-0180*

NANTUCKET WHALING MUSEUM, NANTUCKET

Nantucket was the Houston of its day, back when whale oil lit the lamps and greased the wheels of industry. From the majestic skeleton of a sperm whale to delicate scrimshaw, this unique museum tells of the historical hunt for leviathans and our modern quest to save them. Also on display at this former whale-oil candle factory is the 1849 Fresnel Lens used in Sankaty Head Lighthouse, a restored 1881 tower clock, and an impressive collection of paintings and crafts created by sailors on their whaling voyages. *508-228-1894; nha.org*

A 1849 lighthouse lens at the Nantucket Whaling Museum

Sperm whale skeleton at the Nantucket Whaling Museum

OAK BLUFFS GINGERBREAD COTTAGES, MARTHA'S VINEYARD

In the quiet world of whimsy officially known as the Martha's Vineyard Camp Meeting Association Campground, 19th-century homes outlined in perfectly painted filigree trim are set within a few feet from one another, looking for all the world like an immaculate dollhouse village. Most of the neighborhood's 300-plus "gingerbread" cottages are shuttered during the island winter, but as summer approaches this enchanting community springs to life with walking tours, concerts, visiting speakers, family movie nights, and a world-famous lantern festival, the crowning event of the season. *mvcma.org*

POLLY HILL ARBORETUM, MARTHA'S VINEYARD

On an island known for its preservationist spirit, the Polly Hill Arboretum stands out. This 70-acre plot of walking paths, stone walls, rare trees, and woodlands was the brainchild of the late Polly Hill, a horticulturalist who over the course of 50 years introduced plants and shrubs from around the globe at her West Tisbury property. Today, Hill's vision of a place that is both educational and inspirational endures. For the princely sum of $5, visitors can meander through its forest and meadows and discover the diversity and beauty that Hill spent half a century creating. *508-693-9426; pollyhillarboretum.org*

'SCONSET VILLAGE, NANTUCKET

The village of 'Sconset is both a part of Nantucket and not. A mere 8 miles from the hustle and bustle of the island's center, this former fishing community retains most of Nantucket's older, sleepier charm. The Codfish Park fishermen's shacks are now seaside cottages. There's lunch and ice cream at the 'Sconset Café and snacks at the Siasconset Market. One of the prettiest strolls on the eastern seaboard

is here, too, a bluff walk that takes visitors behind grand homes and alongside towering beach cliffs. When it concludes, you can retrace your steps back to the village center or follow Baxter Road for a postcard-perfect ending at Sankaty Head Lighthouse.

WELLFLEET BAY WILDLIFE SANCTUARY, SOUTH WELLFLEET

Although the interior of Cape Cod is rich with cardinals, mockingbirds, goldfinches, and woodpeckers, it's the coastal birds that draw many visitors here. Shorebirds by the thousands, returning from their Arctic breeding grounds, stop here each fall for much-needed respite and food as they fatten up for their journey south. The Massachusetts Audubon Society, which owns and maintains the Wellfleet Bay Wildlife Sanctuary, claims to have spotted more than 250 different species on that property alone. If birds don't move you, the sanctuary has 5 miles of trail ideal for wandering, and a bench overlooking the water at Goose Pond that's one of the most serene spots on the Cape. *508-349-2615; massaudubon.org*

WELLFLEET DRIVE-IN, WELLFLEET

When the Wellfleet Drive-In opened for business in 1957, the New England landscape teemed with outdoor theaters just like it. Today, the Wellfleet stands as an enduring marker of the era, the Cape's sole remaining drive-in and one of only three left in Massachusetts. The scene is what you'd expect, with kids throwing footballs and Frisbees before dusk, and parents doing a preshow shuffle of lawn chairs and picnic blankets. Line up at the concession stand for the kind of movie fare nobody can get enough of. Then watch as darkness descends, the big screen lights up, and summer feels, well, like summer again. *508-349-7176; wellfleetcinemas.com*

Sankaty Head Lighthouse

SPOTLIGHT ON
BOSTON HARBOR ISLANDS

One of the best-kept secrets in Boston awaits just beyond the skyline, some 30 pristine islands scattered across the 50 square miles of the Harbor. Part of the Boston Harbor Islands National and State Park, they're full of spots ideal for walkers, paddlers, campers, and lovers of history and unexpected scenery. Yet each year only about 130,000 visitors arrive on their shores via ferries.

One of the major deterrents is accessibility. Only 6 of the islands—Georges, Spectacle, Peddocks, Lovells, Bumpkin, and Grape—can be reached by public ferry from the mainland. For those of you who make the effort, however, it's like turning over a rock to uncover a purple starfish. You'll find a surprising blend of old military forts, centuries-old lighthouses, drumlins, and rugged shoreline, guaranteed to entice the budding historian or those of us who yearn for a slice of solitude.

Central to the entire cluster of islands, **Georges Island** is the most civilized, with a snack bar, paved walkways, and the remains of Fort Warren, which served as a Civil War military prison. It also offers a close encounter to Boston Light, standing tall on neighboring Little Brewster Island.

Dating from 1783, it is the oldest continuously manned lighthouse in America.

Spectacle Island had its heyday in the 1840s as a casino and upscale resort, but in the 20th century, it became a dumping ground for Boston's garbage. It might have remained an eyesore if some 6.3 million tons of excavated dirt from Boston's Big Dig hadn't been used to reshape the land and provide topsoil for more than 2,400 trees. Now Spectacle boasts the highest point on the Eastern Seaboard south of Maine and more than 5 miles of trails that lead walkers down to the beach.

The largest island in the group is 210-acre **Peddocks Island**, once home to Fort Andrews, a training facility during World Wars I and II. You can walk around the boarded-up barracks, play a game of croquet on the parade ground, or stroll high above the East Head cliffs to look down at "the Gut," a nasty current between the island and the town of Hull that wreaks havoc on sea kayakers who try to paddle across.

Bumpkin Island likewise offers hiking trails, though some are paved as a result of a children's hospital that stood here at the turn of last century. You can actually explore the hospital's crumbling remains, or the remnants of a 19th-century stone farmhouse. Peddocks and Bumpkin have sites for overnight camping, as does **Grape Island**, which has been used only for agriculture and thus retains a genuine wilderness feel. **Lovells Island** also offers camping, along with a particularly beautiful and peaceful beach not far from the remnants of Fort Standish. Reserve a campsite on one of these islands, and pay a nominal fee—and you, too, can experience the never-to-be-forgotten sight of the sun rising over the Atlantic and setting over the Boston skyline. *617-223-8666; bostonharborislands.org*

Fort Warren on Georges Island

Sailing by Boston Light

SPOTLIGHT ON

TOP 15 MASSACHUSETTS EVENTS

JANUARY

Moby-Dick Marathon

Literary fans, rejoice! The New Bedford Whaling Museum celebrates Herman Melville's *Moby-Dick* with a 25-hour nonstop reading. Drop by for a chapter, or complete the marathon and win a prize. *508-997-0046; whalingmuseum.org*

MARCH

South Boston St. Patrick's Day Parade

Southie shows its pride with one of the largest St. Paddy's parades in the country. Claim a spot along the 4-mile route from West Broadway to Dorchester Street, and you'll encounter bagpipers, military units, bands, clowns, and a bevy of characters to keep you and the kids smiling. *844-478-7287; southbostonparade.org*

APRIL

Patriots' Day

Where better to commemorate Patriots' Day, which marks the Battles of Lexington and Concord and the start of the American Revolution, than on the very ground where so much history happened? Beyond the battlefield reenactments at Minuteman National Park, Lexington, Concord, and the surrounding towns serve up a weekend jam-packed with patriotic fun. *978-369-6993; nps.gov/mima*

MAY

Lilac Sunday

Nothing can quite match the fragrance and beauty of the lilac display, with nearly 400 plants of 176 varieties blanketing Bussey Hill in the 280-acre expanse of Harvard's Arnold Arboretum. Exploding in pinks, lavenders, blues, and whites each May, they've been a Boston mainstay for more than 100 years, and even have their own holiday, Lilac Sunday, which includes performances, picnics, and other family fun. *617-524-1718; arboretum.harvard.edu*

JULY

Boston HarborFest

Featuring hundreds of events highlighting Boston's role in our country's founding, this is America's biggest birthday bash. Events are held around the waterfront and downtown areas and include a Children's Day, a concert series, and Chowderfest, plus walking tours of historic sites, lectures, reenactments, and of course, a fantastic fireworks show. *617-439-7700; bostonharborfest.com*

Lowell Folk Festival

Six stages around the city anchor the largest free folk festival in the country. Traditional music, dance, and storytelling entertain while you enjoy ethnic foods, parades, crafts demonstrations, and games. *978-970-5000; lowellfolkfestival.org*

AUGUST

Feast of the Blessed Sacrament

Billed as the largest Portuguese feast of its kind in the world and the single largest ethnic festival in New England, this annual New Bedford tradition is still going strong over a century later. More than 100,000 people are expected to attend the event, which offers a parade, a carnival midway, Portuguese food and performances, a 5K road race, and a 40-foot barbecue pit. *508-992-6911; portuguesefeast.com*

Grand Illumination Night

The crowning event of the Martha's Vineyard summer season is held in the fairytale Oak Bluffs neighborhood of gingerbread cottages known as the Campground. In a tradition going back more than 140 years, residents decorate their historic cottages with ornate paper Chinese and Japanese lanterns. After a community sing and band concert, wander through the magical wonderland of lights to your hearts' content. *508-693-0525; mvcma.org*

SEPTEMBER-OCTOBER

Topsfield Fair

Held in the North Shore town of Topsfield, the oldest continually operating county fair in America showcases New England's largest apiary exhibition, a fall flower show, draft horses, plenty of farm animals, food, arts and crafts, and nationally-known entertainment. Don't miss the giant pumpkin weigh-in where growers try to beat the world record. *978-887-5000; topsfieldfair.org*

The Big E

Held in West Springfield, the Big E is one of the biggest fairs in North America, and the perfect place to experience all the sights and tastes of the harvest season. Enjoy top-name entertainment, major exhibits, the Big E Super Circus, the Avenue of States, dazzling thrill shows, New England history and agriculture, animals, rides, shopping, crafts, a Mardi Gras parade, and food from around the world. *413-737-2443; thebige.com*

OCTOBER

Head of the Charles Regatta

The site is Boston's Charles River, crowded with 11,000 elite rowers, and 300,000 fans lining the banks, all there for the largest 2-day rowing event in the world. Factor in the views of Boston and Cambridge and the crisp October weather, and it all adds up to an unforgettable New England experience. *617-868-6200; hocr.org*

Haunted Happenings

More than 250,000 visitors flock to Salem for this month-long salute to Halloween and the harvest season. Among the highlights are a grand parade, a street fair, family film nights, costume balls, ghost tours, haunted houses, live music, and harbor cruises. *978-744-3663; hauntedhappenings.org*

NOVEMBER

Cider Days

At Cider Days, you can enjoy orchard tours and workshops at various locales throughout Franklin County, and pay a visit to the marketplace at Shelburne Buckland Community Center to peruse a selection of items from local artisans, producers, and tempting food vendors. Secure tickets in advance for the Cider Salon, which showcases the world's largest selection of hard ciders, all yours for the tasting. *413-773-5463; ciderdays.org*

America's Hometown Thanksgiving Celebration

See the history of Thanksgiving brought to life as Pilgrims, Native Americans, soldiers, patriots, and pioneers climb out of the history books and stride onto the streets of Plymouth. Events include a harvest farmers' market, a historical village, a food festival, concerts, and a "chronological parade" representing the march of time from the 17th through 21st centuries. *508-746-1818; usathanksgiving.com*

DECEMBER

Main Street at Christmas

Head to Stockbridge to see the town made famous by a Norman Rockwell Christmas painting, as it serves up house tours, readings, caroling, and a holiday concert. On Sunday, watch as the scene from Rockwell's painting is re-created, right down to the vintage cars. *413-298-5200; stockbridgechamber.org*

➤ AT HOME WITH GREAT WRITERS

New England is jam-packed with historical bragging rights—not only in the sense that these six little states were (and are) flourishing epicenters of business, food, industry, art, education, and politics, but also in that the monuments to these achievements are closely packed in together physically. In Massachusetts, this can be a special boon for literary fans, with landmarks across the state dedicated to everyone from Herman Melville to W.E.B. du Bois. These include a number of great authors' homes now preserved as museums, allowing visitors to step inside and grasp how passion and place helped shape phrases that still stir our minds and our hearts.

The town of Concord is rife with writers' homes, but none is more iconic than the **Old Manse** (*978-369-3909; thetrustees.org*), the Georgian clapboard house that newlyweds Nathaniel and Sophia Hawthorne rented from the Emerson family in 1842. The house overlooks the North Bridge, where the "shot heard 'round the world" plunged local militiamen into a battle with long-lasting reverberations. The upstairs study, meanwhile, was ground zero for America's philosophical revolution, the Transcendentalist shift in thought. Ralph Waldo Emerson wrote his landmark essay, "Nature," while gazing out at the Concord River, while Hawthorne installed a desk that condemned him to stare, undistracted by nature, at the opposite wall.

Traveling west to Amherst, you can step inside **The Homestead** (*413-542-8161; emilydickinsonmuseum.org*), where poet Emily Dickinson was born in 1830, died in 1886, and famously holed up for most of the years in between. Dickinson's tiny desk was her refuge from strict parents, the ravages of disease, the destruction of the Civil War, and a secret love. Her body of work—1,800 poems—was her therapy. You'll leave having "met" a woman who chose to "dwell in possibility" rather than in a judgmental world not yet ready for her rule-breaking verse.

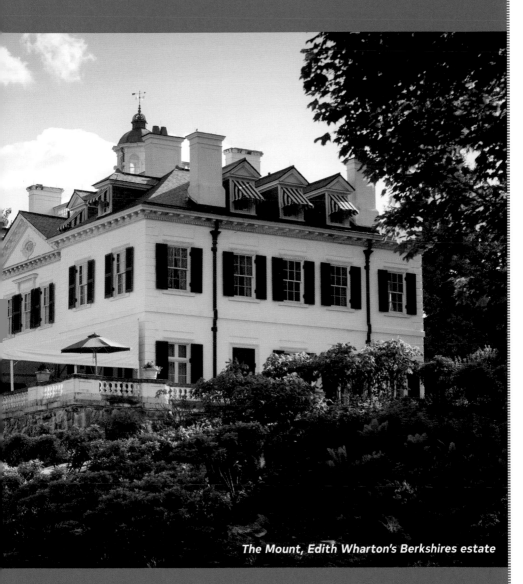
The Mount, Edith Wharton's Berkshires estate

Edith Wharton's Berkshires estate in Lenox, **The Mount** (*413-551-5111; edithwharton.org*), where she lived and wrote from 1902 to 1911, is a testament to how a gracious, thoughtfully conceived home and landscape can be conducive to creativity. She wrote some of the most celebrated of her more than 40 novels here, including *The House of Mirth*. Readings and themed tours ensure that the property is perpetually inspiring.

⇒ MAINE ⇐

VACATIONLAND

————◦————

If foaming waves, rocky shores, and unspoiled wilderness have another name, it's Maine. With a history and culture shaped by the sea, this rugged state has long called to romantics and adventurers alike.

When traveling the coast, you'll feel you're living by the rhythm of the tides, winding through fishing villages past cottages weathered to silvery gray. Lobstermen still prowl these waters, but today's coastal communities are also havens of culture and cuisine. Kennebunkport and Rockport, for instance, are synonymous with presidents, artists, and craftsmen. And in Maine's biggest city, Portland, there's a flourishing food scene filled with standout chefs, brewers, and bakers (who are perennially in the running, it seems, for James Beard Awards).

Inland, you'll discover villages with their own sturdy grace. In the heart of the state, Mount Katahdin looms above Baxter State Park, a spectacular gift from a former governor that now sprawls more than 200,000 acres. Together with the mountains and woods that surround it, this is the place of unsurpassed beauty that so inspired Henry David Thoreau.

No one knows this wilderness like the legendary Maine Guides, who'll take you fishing, kayaking, or whitewater rafting (and maybe even help you spot a moose), upholding a century-old tradition. Another tradition—outlet shopping in places like Kittery and Freeport, home to L.L. Bean—proves that in Maine, old and new New England can happily coexist.

MAINE ESSENTIALS

WOODS & WATERS

BAXTER STATE PARK, MILLINOCKET

Former Governor Percival Baxter donated more than 200,000 acres to establish this park so that Mount Katahdin—the state's highest peak and the northern terminus of the Appalachian Trail—"in all its glory forever shall remain the mountain of the people of Maine." The result is a wild and beautiful destination that occupies the heart of the Maine woods, both geographically and in spirit. Access is by rough road, there are no snack stands or bathhouses catering to pampered travelers, and no pets, RVs, or cell phones are allowed. The jagged peak of Katahdin dominates the landscape, but the lower peaks offer plenty of less daunting trails. For a different adventure, leave enough time for a plunge in one of the park's chilly rivers after your hike. But whatever you do, arrive early, because admission to the park is often limited. *207-723-5140; baxterstateparkauthority.com*

LITTLE LYFORD LODGE & CABINS, GREENVILLE

It's five hours from Boston, Massachusetts, to Greenville, Maine, and another hour beyond on broken paved roads and dirt logging trails to Little Lyford Pond Camps. Originally a logging camp from the 1870s, then a sporting camp, Little

Little Lyford Lodge & Cabins

Taking in the view at Baxter State Park

Lyford is now owned by the Appalachian Mountain Club as a rustic retreat. In the heart of the region known as Maine's 100-Mile Wilderness, the Camps offer 300 acres of forests, ponds, streams, and trails, including access to the Appalachian Trail and Gulf Hagas, a gorge known for its waterfalls. It's all yours to explore when you book a stay at one of the nine private cabins or in the bunkhouse. *617-523-0655; outdoors.org/lodging*

MAINE STATE MUSEUM, AUGUSTA

Outstanding on its own merits, this museum is a great highway break less than two miles off I-95. Beautifully detailed, lifelike exhibits present the variety of Maine landscapes and traditional industries, such as fishing, agriculture, granite quarrying, ice harvesting, shipbuilding, and lumbering. An exhibit dramatizing the area's Native Americans and early European explorers, "12,000 Years in Maine," is itself worth the stop. *207-287-2301; mainestatemuseum.org*

Baxter Peak sign on Mount Katahdin

➡ MAINE'S GREAT NORTH WOODS

For anyone who has lived along the East Coast, where highways connect major urban centers from Maine to Florida in endless stretches of tightly packed buildings and dense traffic, the notion of a place where you could drive for hours at night and not see a light except for the stars seems to belong to the land of myth. And in fact, the 10 million acres of Maine's Great North Woods, populated largely with black bears, moose, deer, coyotes, and wild trout, exists as much in the realm of legend as it does reality.

This swath of woods and waters has long spoken of a landscape vast and free, beyond the constraints and comforts of society. Henry David Thoreau, who visited the Maine wilderness in the mid-1800s, wrote that he found a kind of spiritual purity in the rawness of the land. The region stretching northward from Bangor to the Canadian border also entered our collective imagination in the images of hardy river-drivers striding across log-choked waters in their spiked boots and of Maine Guides sharing their backwoods expertise at old-school sporting camps on spruce-hemmed lakes.

There are many ways to explore Maine's Great North Woods. **Baxter State Park** (*207-723-5140; baxterstatepark.org*), a gift of 201,000 acres from former Governor Percival Baxter to be preserved "forever wild," is home to mighty Mount Katahdin and has long attracted backpackers who want to go where silence is broken only by sounds from the natural world.

On the park's eastern border is the recently designated **Katahdin Woods and Waters National Monument** (*207-456-6001; nps.gov/kaww*), whose 80,000 acres can now be included with any Katahdin adventure; there, nature lovers are just now discovering the untouched beauty of Wassataquoik Stream and Orin Falls, framed by boulders and a forest of pines. The chance to go whitewater rafting from the Forks through the turbulent Kennebec Gorge, or along the West Branch of the Penobscot River with Katahdin looming above, draws people by the thousands (*threeriverswhitewater.org*).

Years of timber harvesting and the rise of summer cabins and vacation homes have encroached upon the sense of true wilderness that could be found a century ago. But if you pitch a tent along the 92-mile **Allagash Wilderness Waterway** (*nps .gov/maac*), or come to Greenville to paddle along the shores of **Moosehead Lake** (*maineoutfitter.com*), you will feel a tug of the wild that will leave you exhilarated. At one of the traditional sporting camps that for 150 years have lured urbanites to the region, the guestbook includes these words left by one young boy: "It must have been the best time that I've really ever had. I saw my first moose and a calf. My grandfather taught me to fly fish. I sure hate to leave."

MOOSE-WATCHING, MOOSEHEAD LAKE

Maine is home to about 70,000 moose, and one of the moosiest zones in the state is the aptly named Moosehead Lake. You can watch for the largest members of the deer family on foot, by boat, via seaplane, or on a guided moose safari. The surest way to spot one of these gigantic animals is a moose-watch cruise with the Birches Resort in Rockwood. The boat captain knows all the secret, pine-shrouded coves where they tend to hang out. *destination moosheadlake.com/moose*

OLD CANADA ROAD SCENIC BYWAY

Calling the Old Canada Road a scenic byway does a small injustice to Route 201's 78-mile drive between Solon and Sandy Bay Township along the Canadian border. The route starts out flanked by rolling farmland, then climbs steadily into com-mercial timberland, the lair of moose and beaver. Past the Forks you can take a quick detour to hike Moxie Falls, then continue past the Appalachian Trail to end at the Canadian border not far from Jackman. This town is one of Maine's famed fishing, hunting, and snowmobiling outposts and home to the venerable lake-island getaway Attean Lake Lodge. You won't be the first to complete this route; Benedict Arnold led troops through this wilderness on his ill-fated mission to sack Quebec in 1775. *oldcanadaroadscenicbyway.com*

Sunset over the Moose River in Jackman

SUGARLOAF, CARRABASSETT VALLEY

Sugarloaf's 4,237-foot summit is Maine's highest skiable peak, offering views of Mount Washington and the other Presidentials, Mount Katahdin, and into Canada. Here you'll find trails across three mountains, 1,240 acres of skiable terrain, 162 trails, three terrain parks including a super and mini-pipe, and 13 operating lifts. Additionally, Sugarloaf serves up the only lift-serviced, above-treeline skiing in the East. Skiing along the trees is special, but skiing above them is a truly unique experience. *207-237-2000; sugarloaf.com*

THE THEATER AT MONMOUTH, MONMOUTH

For summer high culture, it's hard to beat the Theater at Monmouth, Maine's diamond-in-the-rough Shakespearean theater. Monmouth has been staging professional performances of plays by William Shakespeare and other noted dramatists since 1970. You should try to arrive an hour or so early to picnic on the grounds. Even if you're not attending a play, Cumston Hall, the theater's ornate Romanesque Revival home, is worth the trip to this rural village. *207-933-9999; theateratmonmouth.org*

WHITEWATER RAFTING, THE FORKS

When Wayne Hockmeyer guided the first raft-load of thrill-seekers down the roiling Kennebec River in 1976, he started a new way of life in the Forks region of central Maine. The area quickly became New England's epicenter of whitewater rafting, with unique trips down the Kennebec, the Dead River, or the Penobscot. But beware, because this is no Disney set; people some-times topple from the rafts and are forced to swim the turbulent waters to safety. The adrenaline rush in the Forks is for real, and your adventure will be even more memora-ble because of it. *raftmaine.com*

Skiing Sugarloaf is fun for skiers of all ages.

Rafting in The Forks

➡ CANOEING THE ALLAGASH

Mention the Allagash Wilderness Waterway to avid paddlers and they're bound to get dreamy-eyed. The river flows north out of wild and remote headwaters in the north woods of Maine, spreading out through Allagash Lake, Chamberlain Lake, and Eagle Lake, where Thoreau once camped. Below Chase Rapids, the current quickens and the lakes become smaller and farther apart. By the time the Waterway reaches the border of Canada and joins with the St. John, the Allagash runs broad and fast and shallow. For 92 miles this isolated waterway has cut through some of the most beautiful and unforgiving landscape in the lower 48.

On this federally protected National Wild and Scenic River you will slide through early-morning mist on water so smooth it looks like glass, portage over rocky carries, and line the canoe through tumbling rapids. You will spot loons, eagles, otter runs, and the purple-pink of joe-pye weed in blossom, while smelling the sweet scents of wood smoke and fir trees. Some images will never leave you, from the river braiding through grassy marshland at the entrance to Umsaskis Lake to the massive bulk of Katahdin off to the southeast.

Autumn is a particularly good time to canoe the Allagash. The shoreline ablaze with fall color, and blackflies, mosquitos and most other canoers are long gone. You're also more likely to spy moose, since late September to early October is mating season for these majestic creatures. You'll probably spot one of the big males browsing the shores and shallow waters, looking for a mate.

A complete Allagash run can take up to 10 days, which is why many people opt to do it in sections. In planning your trip, be sure to check out the Maine Department of Agriculture, Conservation, and Forestry website. It offers a lot of helpful information on the waterway, including usage rules, maps, and a series of introductory videos. Going with a guide is strongly recommended for newcomers; this is an adventure isolated from civilization and thus from the instant assistance we've all become accustomed to. But no matter how you do it, you'll find a lifetime's worth of memories. *maine.gov/dacf; northmainewoods.org*

Paddling along the Allagash Wilderness Waterway

DOWN EAST & ACADIA

ACADIAN VILLAGE, VAN BUREN

If you hear French spoken in the villages of northern Maine, it's not your imagination. Acadians from Canada were exiled here when the 18th-century British decided they were potential troublemakers, and their descendants still inhabit the gentle valleys of the St. John River. From mid-June to mid-September in Van Buren you can learn much about the heritage and culture of the Maine Acadians at this cluster of 16 buildings, each furnished to display the vanishing lifestyle of this unique culture. *207-868- 5042; themainelink.com/acadian village*

Acadian Village

BOLD COAST TRAIL, CUTLER

The Bold Coast's beauty lies in its lack of polish. It's raw and untamed. There are no fences or signs blaring "Caution!" on the edge of its steep bluffs. Along this 10-mile hiking loop over rugged ocean cliffs and through forests of spruce and fir, nature hasn't been groomed or reduced to some pretty painting for visitors to come and gaze at. This is a place to interact with the land, to pause to smell the wildflowers, to get a little muddy, to work up some sweat, to dangle your feet atop a bluff. It's a bold idea, but if you can slow down enough to do it, you may just discover that there are still spots for true adventure. *207-941-4412; maine.gov*

FISHING IN GRAND LAKE STREAM

The tiny village of Grand Lake Stream lies deep in Washington County, and though only about 100 people live here year-round, it's famous as a freshwater fishing paradise without equal. When timber companies began selling off their holdings, locals and others who loved the waters rallied and formed a trust that protected some 445 miles of shorefront along 60 lakes. The largest concentration of registered Maine fishing guides live here, their hand-built cedar canoes clustered on the town beach landing in a way of life little changed for generations. These guides are married to the lakes—they know the deep holes, the spawning beds, the coves full of weeds and fish. You might catch landlocked salmon, lake trout, smallmouth bass, pickerel, and white

Along the Bold Coast Trail

Puffins

perch. Come here to talk not of sunsets but of strikes and of lures—Hendrickson Hatches, Gray Ghosts, and Mickey Finns—the code names of this tribal gathering. *grandlakestream.org*

PUFFIN-WATCHING, MACHIAS SEAL ISLAND

They don't know they're adorable, but the restoration of these exotic-looking "sea parrots" on secluded islands off the Maine coast has created one of New England's most anticipated eco-tourism trips. One of the best places to see nesting puffins is 20-acre Machias Seal Island in the lower Bay of Fundy. On the island you'll also spot arctic terns, common eider, razorbill, black guillemot, and common murre, while other pelagic species, such as shearwaters and jaegers, are usually seen on the trip out and back. Three licensed tour operators can land here; the shortest and only U.S.-based trip is offered by Bold Coast Charter Co. out of Cutler, Maine. *207-259-4484; boldcoast.com*

RAYE'S MUSTARD MILL, EASTPORT

At the far eastern edge of the state, tiny Eastport was once the sardine capital of Maine. One by one all the canneries closed, but Raye's Mustard Mill, which made mustard for canned fish, remains a proud survivor. And though it's been around since 1900, the current generation of the Raye family continues to tap into the American consumer's insatiable hunger for authentic, quality products. Their smooth and coarse mustards are made using an old-fashioned grindstone out back; ask to tour the mill on days when mustard is in production. At the on-site Pantry Store, stock up on traditional yellow, hot and spicy, and horseradish mustard, along with a variety of other treats. *800-853-1903; rayesmustard.com*

DID YOU KNOW? Chester Greenwood of Farmington, Maine invented the earmuff in 1873, at the age of 15. Farmington's annual Chester Greenwood Day parade is held on the first Saturday in December.

ACADIA NATIONAL PARK'S CARRIAGE ROADS

When people think of Acadia, they usually think of it as a refuge from civilization; it's been viewed as a "wild place" since the first landscape painters from Eastern Seaboard cities ventured here in the 1840s. But Acadia is no more a work of pure nature than Michelangelo's *David* is a block of pure marble. The landscape and our access to it have been subtly crafted by generations of artists who designed and built an extensive network of trails. Today you can enjoy 125 miles of footpaths and 45 miles of carriage roads.

Acadia's carriage roads are rightly famed for their beauty and grace. Broad and well-wrought of finely crushed stone, often edged with boulders, these gently winding roads have a medieval, fairytale-like quality, and you half expect a troop of knights to come galloping along, pennants fluttering. The roads were one of the grand extravagances of the early 20th century, built so that island denizens could drive their horses and buggies out into the wilds, without suffering the indignity of unattractive sights or untidy lanes. Designed for an earlier era, paid for largely by John D. Rockefeller Jr., they weave through forests, along streams, and up hills, with ocean or lake views that blossom with every yard of elevation.

Today the roads feel as though they were designed solely in anticipation of the invention of mountain bikes, perfect for a slow afternoon's pedal. However, you will quickly find they're also perfect for walking. While biking, climbing, and hiking are adventures of the body, walking is more an adventure of the mind, a time when your thoughts can unspool in a leisurely way. Stop to admire the view of Jordan Pond from the carriage road along the base of Penobscot Mountain, and look down. The road was built atop a 20-foot rock wall painstakingly crafted out of a talus slope; the labor to provide you with this simple view seems nearly Egyptian.

Along these gentle carriage roads one thing you will certainly find a perfect blend of nature and culture, the best part of Acadia National Park, and some might say, of New England. *207-288-3338; nps.gov/acad*

ART MUSEUMS, ROCKLAND

Flanked with wooded hills and historic homes, Rockland is a tiny harbor town with a large reputation in the art world. Enter the galleries of the acclaimed **Farnsworth Art Museum** (*207-596-6457, farnsworthmuseum.org*) and see how artists like Rockwell Kent, Marsden Hartley, and Winslow Homer portrayed the rugged Maine coastline. Across the street, a 19th-century Methodist church has been transformed into the museum's **Wyeth Center**, where works by three generations of Wyeths are on display.

Farnsworth Art Museum

In the nearby town of Cushing you can visit the Farnsworth-owned **Olsen House**, the farmhouse that Andrew Wyeth depicted in the background of *Christina's World*. Rockland's cherry on top for art lovers is the new building designed by renowned architect Toshiko Mori that houses the **Center for Maine Contemporary Art**, which has showcased cutting-edge work by Alex Katz, Leah Gaultier, and Kevin Cyr, to name a few. *207-701-5005, cmcanow.org*

BLUE HILL PENINSULA

While several million people visit Acadia National Park each year, relatively few detour southwestward towards the nearby cluster of coastal villages that make up the Blue Hill Peninsula: Blue Hill, Brooklin, Brooksville, Castine, Penobscot, and Sedgwick. You'll need to drive slow on the narrow country roads that wind past artists' studios and bring you to quiet

TRAVEL TIP: On Open Lighthouse Day you can visit over two dozen Maine lighthouses for free (lighthousefoundation.org).

The Olsen House

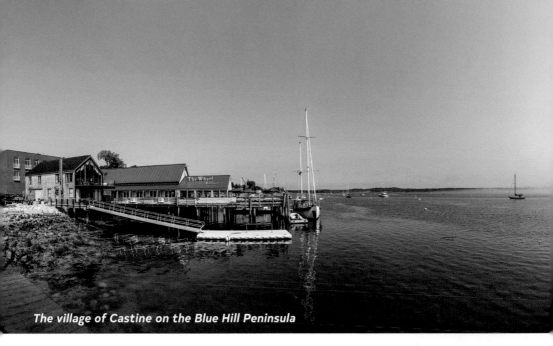

The village of Castine on the Blue Hill Peninsula

coves with views of Mount Desert Island. Maine's peninsulas are known for their serene beauty and feeling of timelessness, and the Blue Hill Peninsula is the best amongst them. Writers from E.B. White and Robert McCloskey to Roger Angell and Michael Chabon agree, and have all drawn inspiration from this landscape. If you're willing to leave the throngs of Acadia and do a bit of exploring, you'll find that inspiration, too. *207- 374-3242; bluehillpeninsula.org*

BLUEBERRY PIE IN MACHIAS

Of all the fine bakeries turning out juicy slices of blueberry pie around coastal and inland Maine, the most sought-after slice can be found at Helen's Restaurant, right in the heart of blueberry country. This Machias institution, which reopened in 2015 after a fire decimated the original diner, folds lowbush wild berries picked just up the road into a flaky crust. You can have your pie in two styles: double-crust or, as many prefer, piled high with fresh whipped cream. (*207-255-8423; helen-srestaurantmachias.com*) And if you're in Machais in August, the town's Wild Blueberry Festival features contests, a quilt

➡ MONHEGAN ISLAND

Everyone who has experienced the special charm of Monhegan Island speaks of it in hushed tones, as if it was sacred ground. And for those who love art, wind-scoured cliffs, and villages that have barely changed in a century, this whale-shaped bit of rock 10 miles out to sea certainly seems worthy of respect. It's not overrun with cars, it's not attached to cable television, it's not a wifi hotspot. The island's isolation from the outside world is what makes it sacred to those in the know.

To get there, drive to Port Clyde and hop aboard the **Monhegan Boat Line** (*207-372-8848; monheganboat.com*), which departs as early as 7 a.m. with a last return at 4:30 p.m., or opt for one of the two other ferries operating from New Harbor and Boothbay. When you land, stay starboard for a view of **Manana Island**, inhabited for decades by Ray Phillips, the so-called "Hermit of Manana," and later by the Bates family, whose children were longtime subjects of painter Jamie Wyeth.

The only motorized traffic you'll encounter on Monhegan is the occasional freight truck on its way to the wharf, and you can't even rent a bike. You'll likely be on foot throughout your visit, so bring proper footwear. And by that we mean *hiking* footwear: More than 17 miles of trails crisscross 480 protected acres, about two-thirds of the island (*monheganassociates.org/the-trail-map*). Moderate hikes include those to **White Head** and **Burnt Head**, both of which level out after initially steep ascents. After walking for 30 minutes through the island's lush interior, you'll be rewarded with clifftop views of the wide and wild Atlantic. For more-experienced hikers the **Cliff Walk** offers a series of dazzling ocean vistas as you circumambulate the island, a rugged tramp that takes several hours, and requires a healthy dose of insect repellant and sure feet.

Visit the Monhegan Lighthouse and Museum

A view of Monhegan Island and Manana Island

When you're ready to refuel, head back to town to score a cappuccino and home-made blueberry muffin at the wharf side café **The Barnacle** (*islandinnmonhegan .com/the-barnacle*). If you're in the mood for seafood, opt for lobster rolls and chow-der at the **Fish House Fish Market** (*facebook.com/pg/fishhousemonhegan*), which also has picnic tables on a small beach from which you can watch kids rowing visitors across to Manana. **The Novelty** (*207-594-4926; monheganhouse.com/the-novelty*), at the base of Horn's Hill, serves pizza, wraps, salads, and very good ice cream.

If you need to cool off, head to **Swim Beach** in the center of town. Be fore-warned, though, because the water is frigid, and the tide runs hard. But if you dare, a bracing dip won't soon be forgotten. And whatever you do, don't go for a swim anywhere else; the currents around the island are no joke. When you've had your fill of walking, eating, viewing, and swimming, stretch out on a west-facing rock for a seaside nap before your boat departs. Unless you want to stay overnight, but for that you'll usually need reservations months in advance.

As you make your way around you'll likely see a few folks set up with easel and paint, rendering an overturned skiff or an old shingled cottage. Many artists hold view-ing hours in their studios; locations and times are posted on bulletin boards around the village. Indeed, since the mid-19th century, artists such as Rockwell Kent, Edward Hopper, and two generations of Wyeths have drawn inspiration from Monhegan's oceanside cliffs, its light, and its rugged beauty. The same cormorant calls of solitude lure the rest of us today. You just have to listen for them. *monheganwelcome.com*

Popham Beach

raffle, live music, performances, a parade, and kids' activities, plus an array of crafters, artisans and food vendors. And of course, tubs of fresh blueberries. *207-255-6665; machiasblueberry.com*

MAINE LIGHTHOUSE MUSEUM, ROCKLAND

Nothing says "Maine" quite like the pinpoints of light shining across the waters to guide fishermen safely home at night. Opened in 2005, the Maine Lighthouse Museum, became the most extensive lighthouse museum in the world through a merger with the American Lighthouse Foundation, formerly of Wells, and the completion of the Maine Discovery Center, the museum's new home. You can appreciate the magnifying power of an incredible collection of giant Fresnel lenses, contemplate sepia photos capturing the lonely life of lighthouse keepers, and press buttons to hear the different tones of fog horns. Rockland's Breakwater Light is visible out the window, and at night, the beacon at Owls Head winks across the harbor. *207-594-3301; mainelighthousemuseum.com*

Maine Lighthouse Museum

DID YOU KNOW? New Gloucester is home to the country's last active Shaker community, Sabbathday Lake Shaker Village. *maineshakers.com*

MCLOONS LOBSTER, SOUTH THOMASTON

Imagine the lobster shack of your dreams, and you'll have a good picture of the family-run McLoons: a tiny red hut perched over the water with a tented patio and picnic tables. Across a small cove, another red building serves as the drop-off point for day boats like the *Four Winds*, whose crew is unloading lobster crates while the *Edith C.* idles behind, waiting for the berth. You couldn't ask for a more perfect setting to enjoy homemade peach pie, coleslaw, burgers, and hot dogs. But the one thing you absolutely must have is the lobster roll, which is the best you'll find in Maine. *207-593-1382; mcloonslobster.com*

POPHAM BEACH, PHIPPSBURG

At the end of one of those fingers of land that dangles off the Maine coast into the Atlantic, Popham is hopelessly exposed to all the elements. There's nothing manicured about this rare spit of sand sandwiched between rocky shores, home to pieces of driftwood, backed by dwarf pines and uprooted trees. Come at low tide, and the grooved sand leads to a tiny island where seagulls have picked over unfortunate crabs, and mussels lie exposed on the kelp. When the water rolls in, kids swim in the surprisingly warm waters of the tidal pool as parents take long beach walks, watching three-masted schooners and lobstermen cruise past pine-studded islands and lighthouses. Let the cool breeze blow through your hair and breathe in the salty air. This is the raw Maine coast you've yearned for. *207-389-1335; maine.gov*

TOBOGGAN CHUTE AT CAMDEN SNOW BOWL, CAMDEN

Winter in Maine has both charms and thrills, as evidenced at Camden Snow Bowl's toboggan chute. It's the site of the U.S. National Toboggan Championships, so this obviously is not your

Sledding at Camden Snow Bowl

neighborhood sledding hill. The chorus of piercing squeals and throaty primal whelps are an involuntary and universal response to New England's longest toboggan chute, a 440-foot straightaway where sleds can reach speeds of up to 30 mph. It's over before you know it; with your heart still in your throat, you may just want to come back for seconds. *207-236-3438; camdensnowbowl.com*

WINDJAMMERS, CAMDEN

The magic of spending a few days on an authentic Maine windjammer is that you see the coast everyone hopes to see but few actually do. These independently owned and operated boats come in all shapes and sizes, from a rare three-masted schooner built in 1900 to haul cargo, to a 1922 racing yacht , to a 1950s ship built especially for windjamming cruises. But all offer an unforgettable maritime adventure. You can raise the sails if you have the energy, or curl up near the bow if you don't. *800-807-9463; sailmainecoast.com*

→ BIRD-WATCHING IN MAINE

Because of its coastal islands and numerous lakes, Maine is one of the best places in North America to watch birds, both migratory guests and local inhabitants. You can start at **Acadia National Park** (*207-288-3338; nps.gov/acad*) on Mount Desert Island, with 47,000 acres of coastline, lakes, marsh ponds, forests, and streams to explore. Not only does its great diversity of plant and animal life include a 338-bird checklist, this is the place to be for warblers, waterfowl, shorebirds, forest birds, and raptors.

Far to the west in Millinocket, **Baxter State Park** (*207-723-5140; baxterstateparkauthority.com*) boasts more than 200,000 acres and four distinct climatic zones supporting hardwoods, boreal forests, and alpine tundra vegetation. There's an amazing amount of bird life here, from waterfowl to warblers to crossbills. Above 3,000 feet on the slopes of Mount Katahdin is prime territory for spotting the Bicknell's thrush.

And finally, along the southern coast, the **Scarborough Marsh Audubon Center** (*207-833-5100; maineaudubon.org*) makes bird-watching easy with exhibits, a nature trail, canoe and kayak rentals, and naturalist-guided and self-guided programs. While exploring Maine's largest salt marsh, be on the lookout for birds of prey, songbirds, and shorebirds like egrets, herons, and glossy ibises.

SOUTH COAST

ALL-NIGHT SHOPPING AT L.L. BEAN, FREEPORT

On a busy Sunday afternoon the crush and din of the L.L. Bean retail flagship resembles that of a discount department store. But if you come in the middle of the night in the middle of winter, when the temperature is dropping to zero and big black clouds are shouldering in across Casco Bay, you will definitely feel the old heart of Maine beating loud and clear. *877-755-2326; llbean.com*

DID YOU KNOW? In Eastport, Maine, you can be the first person in America to see the sunrise.

Portland's Casco Bay Ferry

BOWDOIN COLLEGE, BRUNSWICK

Chartered in 1794, the prestigious Bowdoin College is a public treasure. Its Brunswick campus houses two of Maine's finest museums: the **Bowdoin College Museum of Art**, which boasts one of the oldest art collections in the country, and the **Peary-MacMillan Arctic Museum**, featuring artifacts from alumnai Robert Edwin Peary and Donald MacMillan and their Arctic treks. Try to arrive during the annual **Bowdoin Summer Music Festival**, when talented students, faculty, and guest artists provide the perfect summer soundtrack. *207-725-3375; bowdoin.edu*

CASCO BAY FERRY, PORTLAND

The first ferry to connect Maine's Casco Bay islands to the mainland got under way around 1870, and 8 years later the Casco Bay Steamboat Company became a permanent year-round outfit dedicated to serving the bay's inner islands. Today Casco Bay Lines and its 4 main ferries give the

DID YOU KNOW? Maine has 3478 miles of coastline—more than California!

islands a vital link to the mainland and each other. For visitors, a day of exploration that begins on Chebeague can easily end with cocktails on Great Diamond. Along the way the views of those islands, of the bay, and of the Portland city skyline make this ferry New England's most inexpensive cruise ship. *207-774-7871; cascobaylines.com*

CLIFF WALK, PROUTS NECK

If Winslow Homer was the American Monet, the rocks of Prouts Neck were his lily pads. Less than a half-hour drive south of Portland, this little peninsula was the lens through which the celebrated painter observed powerful gales, dense fog, and window-rattling nor'easters. Thanks to Homer's brother Charles, who donated this path to the public in 1879, you can stroll the same route that the artist traveled almost every day with his terrier, Sam. As the trail starts its ascent, it offers the glorious ocean vistas that inspired the painting *High Cliff, Coast of Maine*; on the way back down is Kettle Cove, where Homer created his last work, *Driftwood*. Accessible to all, the Prouts Neck cliff walk is a glorious gift, allowing anyone to stroll straight into Homer's masterworks.

THE GOLDENROD, YORK BEACH

Walking or driving around York Beach, you're sure to spot The Goldenrod. Look for the kids mesmerized on the sidewalk, staring through windows at the way the taffy machines twist and pull and slice and wrap millions of pieces of saltwater taffy. Some 65 tons of saltwater taffy are produced annually in the front room of this strikingly old-fashioned restaurant, which has roots back to 1896. An argument over the best flavors can occupy a long car ride, while everyone slurps and chews on their favorite piece. *207-363-2621; thegoldenrod.com*

KITTERY TRADING POST, KITTERY

If your trip to Maine involves biking, hiking, kayaking, canoeing, or fishing, this sprawling shop on multiple levels is an ideal first stop after crossing into the state from New Hampshire. The selection here is somewhat more eclectic and diverse than you'll find in the "original" Maine outdoor store in Freeport, with gear for the wilds, as well as flannels and denims for more urban adventures. Just the sight of the light coming out of the huge windows of this gigantic lodge will put you in the mood for exploration. *888-587-6246; kitterytradingpost.com*

The Goldenrod

NUBBLE LIGHT, YORK

In 1977, when *Voyager 1* and *2* blasted off for Jupiter and beyond in search of possible alien life, their capsules carried photos to show what we revered here on Earth. Among those photos: the Great Wall of China, the Grand Canyon, and York's picturesque Nubble Light. Maine boasts more than 60 standing lighthouses, but this one, perched on the rocks of Nubble Island above the shallows of Long Sands Beach, may well be the one we love most.

Maine's southernmost lighthouse is officially called the Cape Neddick Light Station, and along with the keeper's house is on the National Register of Historic Places. Their likenesses are even engraved on York's town seal, as if to say: *Nubble belongs to the country, but here is its home.*

The keepers of the light lived here from 1879 until the last Coast Guardsman left in the summer of 1987, and all felt that this was their calling. They tended the French-crafted Fresnel lens as if it were a child, polishing its light until it shone like gold. Sometimes winter blew fog that blanketed the knoll for weeks at a time, and the keepers knew that the safety of ships depended on keeping Nubble's red light glowing 13 miles out to sea. At dawn, they'd extinguish the light, watch the sun creep over the water, and start their chores.

Nubble Light is at its finest on a blue-sky day when the ocean scent makes mere breathing worth the trip. Head east on Nubble Road off of Long Beach Avenue in York Beach. Stop at tiny Sohier Park and ahead you'll see the gleaming white tower reaching 41 feet high, and beside it the trim red-roofed keeper's house, a few outlying sheds, and a white picket fence that makes it seem as if the lighthouse is standing on a shady neighborhood street. *nubblelight.org*

(This page) *Scenes of Marginal Way*

Stonewall Kitchen

MARGINAL WAY, OGUNQUIT

Ogunquit gets its name from the Algon-quin word for "beautiful place by the sea," which is how native people described this flat, sandy 3½-mile stretch along the southern Maine coast. First, walk the beach to your heart's content, inhaling therapeutic breaths of salty air. But leave some energy for the Marginal Way, a paved 1¼-mile path that leads from the main beach up the rugged cliffs to the shops and seafood restaurants in Perkins Cove. Be sure to take frequent breaks and soak in the views by taking a seat on any of the 30 memorial benches along the way. Out to sea you'll spot sailboats, yachts, and lobster fishermen bobbing in the water. Hungry yet? Dive into the fresh catch at local institution Barnacle Billy's, a favorite of George and Barbara Bush, who reside part-time in nearby Kennebunk-port. *207-646-2939; ogunquit.org*

STONEWALL KITCHEN, YORK

At the no-frills Stonewall Kitchen café just off the Maine Turnpike, you can fuel up with chowder and a sandwich, which should give you plenty of energy to browse the company store afterward. This far-flung enterprise got its start in 1991, when Jim Stott and Jonathan King sold oddball vinegars at the Seacoast Farm-ers' Market. Word got out, and demand grew. And grew. Today their wonderful flavors, such as peach-ginger jam and maple-champagne mustard, are available nearly nationwide, but you'll find even more options at the York flagship store. *800-826-1752; stonewallkitchen.com*

DID YOU KNOW? Maine harvests 90% of the lobster in the country, and it also has more moose per mile than any other state.

SPOTLIGHT ON
MAINE LIGHTHOUSES

Thousands of visitors flock to Maine's lighthouses every year, drawn to these icons. Fewer than two dozen are open to the public and many are not on the mainland, which means that a sightseeing cruise may be your best chance for a great photo. Some lighthouses welcome visitors to their grounds, including Maine's oldest, Cape Elizabeth's iconic **Portland Head Light** (*207-799-2661; portlandhead-light.com*). In Fort Williams Park, just a few miles from downtown Portland, this lighthouse was commissioned by George Washington and still guards the harbor today. After visiting the fine little museum and gift shop in the former keeper's house, you can picnic in the park or stroll the stunning cliff walk.

Featured on the Maine state quarter, New Harbor's 1835 **Pemaquid Point Light** (*207-677-2492. newenglandlighthouses. net*) greets more than 100,000 visitors a year. They come for the astounding scenery and, in summer, the rare chance to climb a lighthouse tower. There's a fishermen's museum on-site, and a one-bedroom apartment in the keeper's house is actually available for weekly vacation rentals.

Just up the coast, Rockland Harbor's **Breakwater Light** (*207-542-7574; rocklandlighthouse.org*) offers the most dramatic of approaches for visitors. You'll hike across the huge granite slabs of the nearly mile-long Rockland Breakwater, completed in 1901, as waves crash and windjammers pass by under full sail.

The easternmost lighthouse in the United States, **West Quoddy Head** (*207-733-2180; westquoddy.com*) is also famous as Maine's only candy-striped beacon, its red stripes meant to help it stand out against snow. Originally built in 1808, this Lubec lighthouse crowns a beautiful

541-acre state park, where you can picnic overlooking Grand Manan Island. Hike the trails over the cliffs and around the bogs as you watch for birds and whales.

Portland Head Light

SPOTLIGHT ON

DINING AROUND PORTLAND

New England is a foodie paradise, with cities and small towns that punch far above their weight at a national level. But people are often surprised that Boston and even Providence don't get the most accolades. Portland is widely acknowledged as the best food town in New England, thanks to a combination of local sourcing from land and sea, a sophisticated populace, and a proud and scrappy community of chefs. Small but mighty, Portland's relative geographic isolation has allowed it to develop its own flavor, independent of the faddish winds swirling through larger cities.

You could do worse than start your culinary odyssey at chef-owner Chris Gould's **Central Provisions** (*207-805-1085; central-provisions.com*), in a 19th-century former storehouse in the Old Port neighborhood. Gould's deft hand with fish shines in crudos and grilled dishes, with local and seasonally flavored butter. Though it is a mostly small-plates concept, full-size entrees like the roast suckling pig will appease misers unused to sharing. They don't accept reservations and waits can be long, so pass the time in the downstairs bar, sampling from their European wine list and selection of local brews.

Two blocks west is **Miyake** (*207-871-9170; miyakerestaurants.com*), the flagship of chef Masa Miyake's mini empire, which offers not only some of the best sushi in New England but also affordable prices that put Boston's top spots to shame. Among the standouts are snapper with cilantro, truffle oil, and *oba* (a minty herb) and the 10-piece chef's choice, *omakase*.

If you want to sample Maine's growing roster of oyster varieties, try **Eventide Oyster Co.** (*207-774-8538; eventideoyster co.com*). Lobster shack classics like rolls, stews, and chowders get a creative update with Asian and Middle Eastern accents at

Pizza from Slab

this nationally acclaimed seafood haven. The brown butter lobster roll is a must-try.

A block away on the north side of Middle Street is **Duckfat** (*207-774-8080; duckfat.com*), where you can find excellent renditions of panini, salads, charcuterie, soup, and milkshakes. Don't miss the Belgian-style frites that are fried in the flavorful fat that give the restaurant its name.

Just to the north up in East Bayside is the **Drifter's Wife**. (*207-805-1336; drifters wife.com*) This small wine bar in the Maine & Loire wine shop specializes in seasonal small plates and naturally fermented wine. Despite a tiny menu of just 7 or so items, dishes like citrus salad with yogurt and cashews make it one of the hottest tables in town.

Back downtown, look for seasonal small plates and quirky wines at **Sur Lie** (*207-956-7350; sur-lie.com*), whose signature fare includes lamb Bolognese with orange zest and duck egg with roasted carrots and caramel. Or if your tastes run towards thick Sicilian pizzas instead, go a block south to

Eventide Oyster Co.

hit **Slab** (*207- 245-3088; slabportland. com*). The key is an oil-enriched crust that bakes up tender and lofty; you may never go back to thin-crust pies again.

For breakfast on the go, head for **The Holy Donut** (*207-775-7776; theholydonut .com*). Founded in 2012 by Portland native Leigh Kellis, this sweet spot has since garnered national attention and opened two more locations. All of the 20-odd flavors here use Maine-grown potatoes in the dough, producing a dunker so light and moist you'll wonder why anyone makes doughnuts without them.

However, the most popular sit-down spot for breakfast might be **Hot Suppa** (*207-871-5005; hotsuppa.com*). This West End eatery brings Southern soul to Down

East, from buttermilk waffles to biscuits and gravy, to surprisingly great bagels.

For lunch, on the other side of I-295 you'll find **Rose Foods** (*207-835-0991; rosefoods.me*), the brainchild of one of the co-owners of Biddeford's acclaimed Palace Diner, Rose Foods brings the upscale-deli craze to Portland with a menu of top-notch lox, bagels, and pastrami.

The list of worthy eateries is long, but these 10 don't-miss destinations should be more than enough to launch your Portland culinary adventures. When it comes to dining here, the most basic questions—where to start and where/when to stop—are the hardest, particularly if you're in for just a weekend and have maybe six meals to ration out. Better visit for a week at least.

SPOTLIGHT ON

TOP 15 MAINE EVENTS

JANUARY

Pies on Parade

Who doesn't love pie? Don your stretchy pants and puffy jacket, shelve the diet, and enjoy your trek through the Rockland and Camden areas, sampling more than 50 pie varieties as you go along. You'll find sweet and delicious fruit pies, savory meat pies, and everything in between, all provided by local restaurants, inns, and businesses. Reserve your ticket early, because this event is popular with locals and tourists alike. *207-596-6611; historicinnsofrockland.com*

FEBRUARY

U.S. National Toboggan Championships

It's true that many folks that come to Maine to compete will be aiming to secure the fastest time down the wooden Jack Williams Toboggan Chute at the Camden Snow Bowl, but other teams will be in it just for the fun. You can usually spot them by their creative team costumes, and their happy-go-lucky attitudes. Come root for the teams in the zaniest outfits, or join the fun with a team of your own. *207-236-3438; camdensnowbowl.com*

JUNE

Maine Whoopie Pie Festival

Head to Dover-Foxcroft to celebrate the state's signature dessert with a day of fun, music, and sweet snacking, as dozens of bakers serve up thousands of whoopie pies. Vote for your favorites in the Big Whoop competition. *mainewhoopiepiefestival.com*

JULY

Moxie Festival

Join in for three days of "wicked cool" Moxie fun, as this most unusual soft drink is celebrated in its home state. Based in Lisbon, this event offers plenty to drink, of course, along with a concert in the park, a car show, a recipe contest, a parade, a 5K race, and more. *moxiefestival.com*

Yarmouth Clam Festival

More than 100,000 visitors come together at Yarmouth's Memorial Green to celebrate a delicious and vast array of food, an entertaining themed parade, firefighters' muster, live music, and fireworks spectacle. Get into the action by entering road, kayak, and bicycle races, or maybe a clam-shucking contest or two. *207-846-3984; clamfestival.com*

AUGUST

Maine Lobster Festival

Rockland's Harbor Park plays host to 5 days of feasting and fun, where more than 20,000 pounds of lobster will be consumed. So, come ready to do your part with steel seafood crackers and skewers in hand. In between meals, take in the coronation of the sea goddess, a parade, live entertainment, Navy ship tours, cooking contests, and plenty more. *207-576-7512; mainelobsterfestival.com*

Great Falls Balloon Festival

More than 40 hot air balloons take flight over Lewiston at dawn and dusk, while balloons tethered and lit with propane called "Moon Glows" are scheduled for Friday and Saturday evenings at Simard–Payne

Memorial Park. Other festivities include food, live music, a carnival, crafts, and fireworks. *207-240-5931; greatfallsballoon festival.org*

Maine Antiques Festival

Vintage items are all the rage at the state's largest antiques event, featuring more than 200 dealers at the fairgrounds in Union. Discover jewelry, maps, prints, folk art, furnishings, ceramics, paintings, and much more. *maineantiquesfestival.com*

SEPTEMBER

Camden Windjammer Festival

Celebrate Maine's maritime heritage with the largest gathering of old-style sailing ships anywhere. The event kicks off with a parade of schooners into Camden's scenic harbor, and continues with maritime-skill exhibitions and contests, a lobster-crate race, and a build-a-boat contest. *camdenwindjammerfestival.org*

Acadia Night Sky Festival

At this community celebration of Acadia National Park's stellar night sky, enjoy activities including guided night hikes, stargazing, lectures, photography workshops, boat cruises, and films at various locations around the park. If you've never seen the Milky Way from the top of Cadillac Mountain here, it is an experience not to be missed. *acadianightskyfestival.com*

OCTOBER

Pumpkinfest & Regatta

At Pinkham's Plantation, Maine Maritime Museum, Boothbay Railway Village, and other Damariscotta locations, you'll find a giant pumpkin contest, pumpkin catapult, pumpkin derby, pumpkin drop, pumpkin pie eating contest, and more! Perhaps you've detected a theme? Don't miss the big pumpkin-boat regatta finale. *207-677-3087; mainepumpkinfest.com*

Fryeburg Fair

Set in the small town of Fryeburg, where pretty farms give way to rolling hills and views of the majestic peaks of the White Mountains, the state's largest agricultural fair has been going strong since 1851. Enjoy the midway, farm museum, and daily live performances. Plus, don't miss Woodsmen's Day, a fair highlight, with competitions such as the Springboard Chop, Women's Underhand Chop, and the Master's Axe Throw. *207-935-3268; fryeburgfair.com*

NOVEMBER

Festival of Lights, Rockland

Santa arrives by boat in Rockland to kick off the festivities, including the lighting of one of the world's largest lobster-trap Christmas trees. You can also enjoy a parade, horse-drawn wagon rides, a bonfire, caroling, special sales and refreshments offered by downtown merchants, and much more. *207-593-6093; rocklandmainstreet.com*

DECEMBER

Christmas at Victoria Mansion

Local designers deck the halls of Portland's stately historic landmark in this annual highlight of the city's seasonal traditions. Step back into the Victorian era and enjoy the lavish decorations and guided tour. *207-772-4841; victoriamansion.org*

Sparkle Weekend

Come to Freeport during the holidays for the concerts, the dynamic music and light shows, the horse-drawn carriage rides, craft fairs, parade, visits with Santa, and the town's famous talking Christmas tree. Take in a show at the holiday movie marathon, or climb aboard the Amtrak Downeaster for a reading of *The Polar Express*. While in town, wrap up that holiday gift-buying at the many wonderful shops, including that 24/7 mecca, L.L. Bean. *207-865-1212; sparklecelebration.com*

NEW HAMPSHIRE

THE GRANITE STATE

When the glaciers that once blanketed the Northern Hemisphere receded 10,000 years ago, they left New Hampshire with wonderful parting gifts: majestic mountains with jagged notches, tremendous boulders, plunging waterfalls, fertile valleys, and lakes almost too numerous to count. (Except there *is* an official count: 944.) Factor in 18 miles of seacoast, and your New Hampshire vacation photos can have practically any backdrop you choose.

Beyond these natural wonders, the Granite State is also home to some of New England's most distinctive attractions. Hop aboard a train that's been climbing Mount Washington since 1869, or pull up a chair at a historic family restaurant that serves Thanksgiving dinner every day of the year. Walk around the nation's last surviving textile mill village, or zip down the most scenic Alpine ski run in the East. Maybe best of all: Indulge in tax-free shopping everywhere you go.

And by the way, don't be deterred by the state's pugnacious "Live Free or Die" motto. It won't be long into your visit before you discover, in fact, that New Hampshire has some of the most welcoming folks around.

NEW HAMPSHIRE ESSENTIALS

WHITE MOUNTAINS & NORTH WOODS

AMC HUTS, WHITE MOUNTAINS

The roots of the Appalachian Mountain Club run deep throughout in New England. Founded in Boston in 1876 by an intrepid MIT professor, the outdoors group helped map the White Mountains and build what would become the nation's oldest network of hiking huts, winding from Lonesome Lake in Franconia Notch to Carter Notch in the Mountain Washington Valley.

Trekking to an overnight in one of these 8 backcountry aeries lets you connect with that legacy, along with fellow outdoors lovers. More important, spending a night in the Whites is a way to experience them not as majestic, far-off, exotic mountains but as something familiar, perhaps something much like home. *617-523-0655; outdoors.org*

CONWAY SCENIC RAILROAD, NORTH CONWAY

From the 1874 Victorian railway station in North Conway, set off on historic routes in vintage rail cars, while sitting down to an elegant meal or just staring open-mouthed out the windows. Of the railway's 3 routes through the Mount Washington Valley, the 5-hour round-trip excursion through Crawford Notch is the one that we recommend. From the moment the diesel electric locomotive chugs out of the station in North Conway, you'll be treated to the most stunning scenery visible from a train in the Northeast. *800-232-5251; conwayscenic.com*

FLUME GORGE, LINCOLN

The Flume Gorge is what nature looks like in our dreams. Wooden walkways guide you through an 800-foot-long series of waterfalls that crash through this narrow crack in Mount Liberty, raising clouds of mist that float up to the forest floor 90 feet above. It's easily the most enchanted spot in the already enchanted Franconia Notch, which features several magical lakes, the Old Man of the Mountain historic site, and innumerable waterfalls tumbling down the steep sides of Cannon and Lafayette Mountains. *603-745-8391; nhstateparks.org*

(Left) Flume Gorge in Franconia Notch

Lake of the Clouds Hut on the slopes of Mount Washington.

Conway Scenic Railroad

JOURNEY TO THE TOP OF NEW ENGLAND

As the highest peak in the Northeast, Mount Washington claims some of the world's worst weather and the second-highest wind speed ever recorded. It also has some of the best views to be had in New England—that is, when the summit isn't actually enveloped in clouds. On a fair-weather day, visibility can stretch all the way to New York's Adirondacks. But first, you have to get up there.

The method most people use is by car. A drive up the **Mount Washington Auto Road** (*603-466-3988; mtwashingtonautoroad.com*) is an experience that sticks with you for life—as does the iconic "This Car Climbed Mt. Washington" bumper sticker you'll earn. For passengers, it's the breathtaking views that will never be forgotten; for drivers, it's the challenge of maneuvering nearly eight miles up a narrow, guardrail-free mountain road. Needless to say, the Mount Washington Auto Road is not for the faint of heart, but it's an adventure worth every hair-raising minute. The road is open from May to October, weather permitting, and in winter you can ascend to the tree line, if not the summit itself, by way of SnowCoach.

Another exciting option is to take **The Mount Washington Cog Railway** (*603-278-5404; thecog.com*), the jiggling, chattering antique train that's a durable testament to the ingenuity and perseverance of one man. Locals derided New Hampshire native Sylvester Marsh's "crazy" plan to go more than 3 miles and 3,600 feet up 6,288-foot Mount Washington, but on July 3, 1869, Marsh proved the doubters wrong. Today, from late April through November, a little fleet of coal-fired and biodiesel locomotives still use "cog" (or toothed) gears to push 70 passengers at a time at a slow crawl up America's only mountain cog railway. At the steep, 37-degree incline of "Jacob's Ladder," the front end of the passenger car is 15 feet higher than the back. On a clear day the views are stupendous as the trestle tracks carry the locomotives 1,000 feet above the Burnt Ravine, and then up the rocky, barren shoulders of the Presidential Range. A visit to the mountaintop observation station is included in your fare.

Finally, for those of you in good physical condition, you can ascend Mount Washington by one of its many trails. But be warned, hiking a peak that's famously known for its extreme weather is not to be taken lightly; a display at the visitors center atop the summit lists more than 130 fatal mishaps, many involving hikers and climbers. Tackling the mountain on foot should begin by consulting with the **Appalachian Mountain Club** (*617-466-2721;outdoors.org*) for trail conditions and weather. Guidebooks and maps can be purchased online, and expert-led treks are also available. For do-it-yourselfers, there are a number of fine trail options. On the east side, the Tuckerman Ravine Trail is a popular route to the top, and considered "easy" compared to the others. The longer Boot Spur Trail offers better views, as does the more strenuous Lion Head Trail. From the south, the Crawford Path, the oldest continuously used footpath in America, leads to a stunning ridgeline with views of the Ammonoosuc and Tuckerman ravines. However, that is a longer route that may take you all day, so a reservation on one of the buses will get you to the bottom before nightfall.

On the porch of the Mountain View Grand

Cross-Country Skiing in Jackson

Kancamagus Highway

DID YOU KNOW? Born to a poor New Hampshire farm family in 1907, Earl Silas Tupper became a plastics chemist and invented the airtight, watertight lid that made "Tupperware" such a hit.

GRAND HOTEL PORCHES, BRETTON WOODS/WHITEFIELD

Here is the picture to hold: It is nearing twilight in the White Mountains. It doesn't really matter if you're sitting in one of those made-to-pass-the-day chairs on the 900-foot-long veranda of the **Omni Mount Washington** (*603-278-1000, omnihotels. com*), in Bretton Woods, or on the porch of the **Mountain View Grand** (*855-837-2100, mountainviewgrand.com*), in Whitefield. Both of these historic grand hotels understand the beauty of repose, of having the time to simply watch (preferably with a late-afternoon adult beverage in hand), the mountains seemingly close enough to converse with. And ah, the quiet.

SKIING IN JACKSON

Peer up from the Jackson town green and the panorama of peaks is mesmerizing. But don't fall into a trance, venture out to one of the numerous trails maintained by the Jackson Ski Touring Foundation. This nonprofit organization keeps most of its nearly 100 miles of trails well-groomed and ready for beginner or expert snowshoeing, classic track skiing, or skate skiing. Feel free to bring your own equipment or rent it from the foundation's base lodge, where day passes are available for purchase. Follow the tracks of a moose into the deep forest, breathe in the scent of pines, and feel the crisp, clean air of winter. *603-383-9355; jacksonxc.org*

KANCAMAGUS HIGHWAY

Highways usually tell us to speed up, that the destination is the goal and the asphalt is merely an effortless way to get there. Not so on the Kancamagus Highway, affectionately nicknamed "the Kanc." Running from Lincoln to Conway, these 34 miles of pavement twist through the White Mountain National Forest, which is laced with waterfalls, rivers, and mountain vistas. With scenic turnouts, a lovely covered bridge, hiking trails, and rustic campgrounds along the road's length, you could spend hours, even days, enjoying its full measure. *kancamagushighway.com*

TRAVEL TIP: If you're driving the Kancamagus Highway, take advantage of one of the many pullovers to stop and enjoy the tumbling Swift River and its endless series of waterfalls.

TOP SCENIC DAY HIKES
IN THE WHITE MOUNTAINS

Most of us are not quite ready for a week-long tramp of the White Mountain backcountry, and even if we are, it's nice to take a day hike once in a while. Beginners should start on the **Mount Willard Trail**, a 3.2-mile round trip that starts in the lofty notch near the source of the Saco River, close to the train depot and Appalachian Mountain Club's Highland Center. Soon you'll hike along the ledges of this small Willey Range peak, enjoying the eagle's-eye view of a U-shaped valley. You'll finish at an open perch showcasing the towering Webster Cliffs, historic Willey Slide, and more.

Another moderate hike is the 4.4-mile **Welch-Dickey Loop Trail**, going over two low-lying mountains near Waterville Valley. This splendid loop features Mad River Valley vistas, mostly forgiving hiking, and incredible ledges. There's some rock scrambling, but the eye candy is worth it.

For something a little more challenging, try the 6.6-mile round trip **Edmands Path and Mount Eisenhower Loop**, which will take you up the 4,760-foot Mount Eisenhower in Chandler's Purchase. It's a taxing trek, but generally offers fine footing before the steep push to its flat, bald crown. The awe-inspiring view takes in fellow outlying Presidential Range jewels. To the south through Crawford Notch and east along the Kancamagus Highway to Albany, the **Champney Falls Trail** takes you a healthy 7.6 miles up Mount Chocorua. With a multitude of exacting trail choices, paths lead to the bare 3,500-foot summit showcasing the vastness of the Whites and beyond. This is a wonderful vantage point to see Mount Washington and the unspoiled Sandwich Range Wilderness.

To the west, the classic **Franconia Ridge Loop** of the Old Bridle Path, Falling Waters, Franconia Ridge, and Greenleaf Trails is 9 miles of pure heaven for those of you in good shape. Arduous and wonderful, the traverse over Little Haystack, Mount Lincoln, and Mount Lafayette is a classic high-wire circuit, with a healthy share of the trip above treeline. Completing this hike will make you feel like you've made it into the big leagues, and you have.

As always, even on a day hike, be cognizant of exposure to weather. If you stay prepared and alert, you can enjoy the glories of the White Mountains without succumbing to their dangers.
visitwhitemountains.com

LAKE UMBAGOG WILDLIFE PADDLE, ERROL

Grab a canoe from a local outfitter and put in north of Errol on Route 16 to find out why Lake Umbagog was named a National Wildlife Refuge. Loons, Canada geese, and herons lounge in the waters of this pristine lake on the Maine border, while moose and even the occasional black bear will show up. And yet it's the bald eagles that keeps folks coming back. A short paddle on the Androscoggin River brings you to a deserted island. Every year since 1989, a family of eagles has given birth in springtime to their young in a large nest atop a dead tree. *603-538-6707; nhstateparks.org*

LIMMER'S, INTERVALE

In a large green barn in the shadow of the White Mountains, Peter Limmer and Sons still build their famous custom hiking boots just the way they did when they first opened their doors in 1950. They use handcrafted, fine-grain leather, with single-seam uppers to craft what many people say are the finest boots in the world. The backlog means you have to wait a good 18 months for your boots, but there's a reason why hikers come here from as far away as Tanzania for their footwear. *603-356-5378; limmercustomboot.com*

Birdwatching on Lake Umbagog

Canoe on Lake Umbagog

Zeb's General Store

POLLY'S PANCAKE PARLOR, SUGAR HILL

Do you like pancakes, views, and most especially views of pancakes? Then you'll be in blueberry buckwheat heaven at this family-owned institution, which has been flipping delectable discs for more than 75 years. Polly's has come a long way from its humble beginnings in a woodshed. They inaugurated a new building in 2015 to accommodate the 58,000 pilgrims who make the trek to tiny, aptly named Sugar Hill each year. *603-823-5575; pollyspancakeparlor.com*

SHOPPING IN NORTH CONWAY

With 70 brand-name outlets at Settlers Green and Settlers Crossing, North Conway is the premier shopping destination in the Whites. Even better, just up the road from the outlets you'll find a town center studded with independently owned shops, like Zeb's General Store, with its 67-foot-long candy counter and 5,000 New England–made products. And the 5&10 Cents Store is the real thing, run by the same family since 1931. *603-356-7011; northconwayvillage.net*

THE FROST PLACE, FRANCONIA

Robert Frost's farmstead overlooking the White Mountains was his home during the period when his poetry first began to attract international attention. Two rooms of the modest 19th-century dwelling house a museum of his life and work, including letters and signed first editions of his books. The rest is now the Center for Poetry and the Arts, which hosts a poet-in-residence each summer and sponsors special programs. Nearby, the half-mile Poetry-Nature Trail matches 16 of Frost's poems with the Franconia settings that inspired them. *603-823-5510; frostplace.org*

DID YOU KNOW? New Hampshire has a zero percent sales tax. Enough said!

Skier on Polecat, Wildcat Mountain

DID YOU KNOW? In New Hampshire, and other parts of New England, a water fountain is often called a "bubbler."

THE ROCKS ESTATE, BETHLEHEM

Balsam firs stretch to the horizon at the 1,400-acre Rocks Estate, a Christmas tree farm extraordinaire in the White Mountains. It was the former home of International Harvester cofounder John Jacob Glessner, and though the 2 mansions on the property are long gone, many historic buildings remain amongst the web of trails. Glessner's heirs deeded the estate to the Society for the Protection of New Hampshire Forests, which today offers tours, carriage rides, and programs on everything from vernal pools to wild turkeys to maple sugaring. *603-444-6228; therocks.org*

WILDCAT MOUNTAIN SKI AREA, PINKHAM NOTCH

There are higher peaks and steeper trails throughout New England. But the summit of Wildcat Mountain gives a sense of the wild Northeast like no other place can. Polecat, the most scenic Alpine trail in the country, cuts down Wildcat's flank. It's a green-dot trail for beginners all the way, and for more than 2 miles, you look west into Mount Washington's rugged Tuckerman Ravine. Legendary north country skiers cut the trails on Wildcat, and they knew what they were doing. No trail in New England is more loved by those who know it than Polecat. *603-466-3326; ski-wildcat.com*

DID YOU KNOW? West Ossipee resident V.D. White invented the snowmobile in 1913 by adding caterpillar treads to a Ford.

LAKES & CENTRAL

CANTERBURY SHAKER VILLAGE, CANTERBURY

At Canterbury Shaker Village, you will not only learn history, you will experience its living endurance. The Shaker sect believed in simplicity, equality of sexes, communal living, pacifism, celibacy, and respect for nature, and the 300 people who lived and worked here two centuries ago would still feel at home all these decades later. Decades after the last Shaker sister at Canterbury died, the village remains a tribute to a way of life that influenced generations to appreciate the beauty in simplicity. *603-783-9511; shakers.org*

CASTLE IN THE CLOUDS, MOULTONBOROUGH

When it was the home of manufacturing tycoon Thomas Plant in the first half of the 20th century, this mountaintop baronial estate was called Lucknow. Today it's better known as Castle in the Clouds, and is maintained along with some 5,380 acres and 28 miles of trails by the Castle Preservation Society and the Lakes Region Conservation Trust. The Tiffany glass, the well-stocked library, the big billiard table, the guest room Teddy Roosevelt slept in—it's all still there, along with the finest views from any house in New Hampshire. *800-729-2468, castleintheclouds.org*

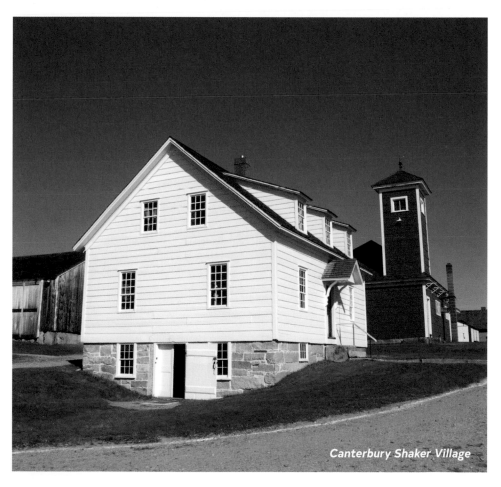

Canterbury Shaker Village

Castle in the Clouds

➡ TOWERING ABOVE THE TREE LINE

The view from the Milan Hill fire tower extends for 100 miles. From the tower's viewing platform, the blue-green North Woods roll endlessly north into Quebec, while to the south majestic Mount Washington and her sisters reach for the sky. This turret outside Berlin is only one of New Hampshire's 16 active fire towers, remnants of an era when dozens of overlooks stood guard from Maine to Rhode Island. Fifteen of these are open for you to enjoy their unique history and spectacular views.

In the late 1800s, heavy logging and widespread forest fires created a definite need for New Hampshire's fire lookout towers. By 1909, using a firefighting-budget surplus, the state bought telephones and fixtures for 5 towers. Encouraged by assistance from timber owners and the Appalachian Mountain Club, the state was operating a network of 29 lookouts by 1917. A century later, aerial surveillance and telecommunications have eclipsed the golden age of fire lookouts, but the remaining towers still provide important coverage.

You can reach them via a short drive, a gentle walk, or a moderately strenuous hike. Among the most challenging to reach on foot is the tower atop 2,937-foot high **Mount Kearsarge** (*603-526-6168; nhstateparks. org*). The summit tower is best appreciated as part of a 2.8- mile loop hike from Winslow State Park, going up the rocky Wilmot Trail and following the gentler Barlow Trail down.

Other especially scenic towers include Gilford's **Belknap Mountain** (*belknaprangetrails.org*) fire tower, which sits atop a 2,384-foot summit and looks over Lake Winnipesaukee. The tower is accessible by a couple of foot trails, each of them less than a mile long. **Blue Job** (*firelookout.org/lookouts/nh/blue-job*) in Farmington is pronounced like the biblical figure, in case you're asking for directions. Its only 1,356 feet high, but is so prominent above the surrounding land that the view extends from Mount Washington's lofty peak to the Isles of Shoals and, on a clear day, to Boston's John Hancock Tower. A couple of ½-mile paths through fields of blueberries lead to the summit.

Mount Cardigan (*outdoors.dartmouth.edu/activities/hiking*) in Orange scarcely needs a tower, because its bare 3,121-foot summit provides sweeping views. A 1.4-mile trail from Cardigan State Park's auto road is a great first hike for families with a taste for a true mountain experience. An even easier summit is the state's only stone lookout tower on **Mount Prospect** (*nhstateparks.org*) in Lancaster, with a 1½-mile auto road that doubles as a walk.

In some cases, these fire towers provide the only possible view from some of New Hampshire's famously wooded summits. Their viewing platforms are the perfect settings for panoramic vistas, romantic rendezvous, or just a bit of perspective.

Loons

→ HART'S TURKEY FARM

For over six decades family-run Hart's Turkey Farm has been an integral part of the community of Meredith. In the late 1940s, brothers Russ and Larry Hart moved with their wives from New Jersey to New Hampshire and began raising turkeys, chickens, vegetables and fruits that they sold from a truck. They soon opened a 12-seat eatery, which gradually expanded into the nearly 500-seat restaurant of today, located just below the junction of Route 104 and Route 3.

The Hart philosophy—"If you want it done right, do it yourself"—is evident in the quality of their classic turkey dinner, popular not only at Thanksgiving, but year-round. Almost everything is made on the premises, including the carrot relish, salad dressings, whipped potatoes, soups and rich chowders, premium ice cream, and, of course, tender roasted turkey. Turkey plates are available in 3 sizes, up to the jumbo with more than a pound of turkey. For those with a slightly more modest appetite, there are a variety of sandwiches, from turkey meatball subs to turkey Reubens to traditional Gobblers, embedded with cranberry, stuffing and mayo. Turkey tempura, turkey nuggets, and turkey pot stickers might tempt you, too.

No visit to the lovely lake town of Meredith is complete without a visit to this iconic symbol of hospitality. At holiday time, hundreds of meals are ordered for take-out alone, so you should phone ahead. As the locals say, "See you at Hart's." *603-279-6212; www.hartsturkeyfarm.com*

HOOD MUSEUM OF ART, HANOVER

Dartmouth shares one of the largest college art collections in the U.S. without charging a dime. From ancient Egyptian and Mesopotamian artifacts to Italian Renaissance sculpture to paintings by Picasso, 65,000 pieces are housed in the school's small but outstanding fine arts

museum. Across the green in the Baker Library is a phantasmagorical multi-panel mural by Mexican artist José Clemente Orozco, an artist-in-residence at Dartmouth in the early 1930s. *603-646-2808; hoodmuseum.dartmouth.edu*

LOON CENTER AND MARKUS WILDLIFE SANCTUARY, MOULTONBOROUGH

On the shores of Lake Winnipesaukee, the Loon Center honors the speckled and spectacular lake denizen with an interpretive center and a sanctuary with more than 200 acres of woods, marshes, ponds, and streams. Easy walking trails abutting the water offer ample opportunity to see and hear the resident loons. Don't miss the Loon's Feather gift shop, where your dollars go to support the protection and preservation of loon nesting areas. *603-476-5666; loon.org*

M/V *MOUNT SUNAPEE II*, SUNAPEE HARBOR

History floats on this classic 90-minute narrated tour of Lake Sunapee, sure to be one of your favorite family cruises. Along the way you'll learn about the charming harbor and the spiritualists who camped out at Blodgett Landing in the 1800s. Kids often get to steer the ship as it cruises the 10-mile-long mountain lake, past 8 islands and 3 lighthouses. Don't worry, there's plenty of leeway if they should take a wrong turn. *603-938-6465; sunapeecruises.com*

Kayaking on Squam Lake

SAINT-GAUDENS NATIONAL HISTORIC SITE, CORNISH

The great American sculptor Augustus Saint-Gaudens was the brightest star of Cornish, New Hampshire's art community from 1885 until his death in 1907. His regal home, Aspet, and its art-filled gardens, evoke the man who crafted both outstanding public monuments, such as the Robert Shaw Memorial on Boston Common, and small things of great beauty, like the $20 gold coin for the U.S. Treasury. *603-675-2175; nps.gov/saga*

SQUAM LAKE

Thirty years ago, when Hollywood came to New England to find a hauntingly beautiful location to film *On Golden Pond*, they chose Squam Lake. With its islands, coves, and miles of shoreline, Squam was seemingly unchanged by time, and it remains magical and moving today. At the Squam Lakes Association in Holderness, you can rent a canoe, kayak, or sailboat and even get instruction from the people who for a century have kept Squam golden. *603-968-7336; squamlakes.org*

SOUTH & SEACOAST

AMERICAN INDEPENDENCE MUSEUM, EXETER

Although no revolutionary blood was shed on its soil, the Granite State was no mere spectator to the birth of our country. Exeter's Ladd–Gilman House was the home of New Hampshire's first political family, and now The Society of the Cincinnati runs a museum chronicling the considerable contributions of the state's founding fathers. On display are military ephemera, furniture, and an impressive collection of documents, including seasonal attractions like an original broadside of the Declaration of Independence and two drafts of the Constitution. *603-772-2622; independencemuseum.org*

Examples of sculptor Augustus Saint-Gaudens's smaller-scale work can be found throughout the Saint-Gaudens National Historic Site.

CANOBIE LAKE PARK, SALEM

From its early days as a "pleasure resort" in 1902, with canoeing and a botanical garden, Canobie Lake has evolved into a classic New England amusement park with actual fear-factor ratings. Its 85 rides, games and attractions include thrill rides, such as the Corkscrew Coaster and the Starblaster, a shuttle lift-off meets bungee jumping that demands intrepid commitment. Those of us who like a slower pulse rate can stick with family rides like Crazy Cups and Dodgem bumper cars. *603-893-3506; canobie.com*

DOWNTOWN PORTSMOUTH

Founded in 1623, Portsmouth is the third oldest town in the country, and unquestionably one of the most beautiful. It is also one of the most walkable, with trendy side streets brimming with cafés, craft breweries, shops, and restaurants. The Piscataqua River slices alongside Prescott Park, alive with summer jazz, "chowdah" fests, boat cruises, and outdoor movies. Wannabe time travelers can duck into Strawbery Banke Museum to breathe some 18th-century air in this 10-acre spread of historic houses. Nearby, the African Burying Ground Memorial Park on the Portsmouth Black Heritage Trail honors those too often forgotten by American history. *603-610-5510; goportsmouthnh.com*

Historic Portsmouth in winter

→ DINING IN PORTSMOUTH

Portsmouth is New Hampshire's hippest town, with a food scene that hits every note, including hyperlocal oysters, small plates, and foraged fare. It's also geographically condensed, with many worthy eateries jammed into the historic core of the town.

At **Moxy** (*603-319-8178; moxyrestaurant.com*), Chef Matt Louis does global small plates with a New England accent, with hasty pudding frites, whoopie pie sliders, and a tasting flight of Granite State beers served in 5-oz. canning jars. A block away at Chef Evan Mallett's **Black Trumpet Bistro** (*603-431-0887; black trumpetbistro.com*) you can nibble on sustainable seafood and seasonal fare with Latin and Mediterranean accents. We recommend anything with mushrooms or other foraged, wild-harvested treats, such as dandelion greens and balsam.

In the center of the historic district, **Franklin Oyster House** (*603-373-8500; franklinoysterhouse.com*) offers seafood tapas and large plates from the team behind Moxy. Can't miss dishes include any of the small plates listed under "Sea Fare." A block to the north you'll find another seafood haven, **Row 34** (*603-319-5011; row34nh.com*). This wildly popular Boston oyster house serves both "creamy" Maine-style lobster rolls, and buttered Connecticut-style rolls. Both variations are amazing, as are the "Row 34" Duxbury oysters.

More seafood delights can be found at **Jumpin' Jay's Fish Café** (*603-766-3474; jumpinjays.com*). This granddaddy of gourmet Portsmouth seafood has been raising the bar since 2000, and features some of the best crab cakes in New England. But if a gastropub is what you're looking for, try **Earth Eagle Brewings** (*603-502-2244; eartheaglebrewings.com*). Microbrews are king in Portsmouth, and Earth Eagle offers both the joy of at-the-source imbibing with an inspiring gastropub menu, including heavenly house-made soft pretzels.

If you're looking for breakfast, perhaps you should try **La Maison Navarre** (*603-373-8401; mnpastry.com*) on Congress Street. This chic bakery is as close to a modern Parisian patisserie as you'll find on the East Coast, and owners Charlotte Reymond and Victor Navarre are French expats and masters of the macaroon. Next door is **The Friendly Toast** (*603-430-2154; thefriendlytoast.com*), a perpetual retro breakfast favorite. Don't miss the coconut pancakes and the egg scrambles.

And finally, near the Portsmouth Museum of Art, you will find **Street** (*603-436-0860; streetfood360.com*). With a menu inspired by global street food, this sunny spot serves up sharable plates of fried cauliflower in tamarind glaze, empanadas, bibimbop, and yucca fries.

HARRISVILLE DESIGNS, HARRISVILLE

Back in the early 1970s, the looms fell silent in this classic New England mill town. Then a descendant of the Colony family that had operated the mills for generations helped convert the brick structures into shops, offices, and lodgings. As the only surviving textile mill village in the United States, this site by a peaceful millpond is now a National Historic Landmark. Housed in a former 1850s wool storehouse, Harrisville Designs attracts visitors for its fine, handmade weaving accessories and crafts workshops. While you're here, don't miss the gourmet goodies at the Harrisville General Store. *800-338-9415; harrisville.com*

Floor Loom in the Harrisville Designs studio

ISLES OF SHOALS STEAMSHIP CO., PORTSMOUTH

Part of the cluster of 9 scenic, rocky islands that compose the Isles of Shoals, Star Island lies some 10 miles out from Portsmouth Harbor. You'll arrive aboard the *Thomas Laighton*, a three-decker ferry, and then disembark onto a rock-strewn, sea-splashed nugget. On a hot, blue-sky day, spend your time on the island exploring, or give yourself the shivers by reading Anita Shreve's *The Weight of Water*, a historical novel about the real-life double murder that took place on nearby Smuttynose Island in 1873. *603-431-5500; islesofshoals.com*

MOUNT MONADNOCK

From the summit of the free-standing Mount Monadnock, see what Mark Twain and Henry David Thoreau saw on a clear day: all 6 New England states. Routes include the meandering Pumpelly Trail near the shores of sparkling Dublin Lake, or the popular White Dot Trail from Monadnock State Park in Jaffrey. This 3,165-foot peak wasn't born bald, but early settlers denuded it when they burned out the packs of wolves inhabiting the summit. Ever since, its lovely views and 40 miles of trails have fired the imaginations of artists, writers, and more hikers than almost any other mountain in the world. *603-485-1031; nhstateparks.org*

THE MUSIC HALL, PORTSMOUTH

This elegantly rehabbed Portsmouth hall hosts an astonishing range of performers, from Tom Brokaw to Melissa Etheridge, but that seems quite appropriate for an 1878 Victorian theatre that once hosted vaudeville acts. Its acclaimed "Writers on a New England Stage" series has seen the kind of celebrity cross-pollination that would thrill any reader, from Salman Rushdie to Patti Smith. Across the street, "Writers in the Loft" hosts more-intimate programs and signings featuring best-selling authors such as prolific Vermont novelist Chris Bohjalian. *603-436-2400; themusichall.org*

White Island Lighthouse, an Isles of Shoals landmark

Portsmouth Harbor tugboats

ODIORNE STATE PARK, RYE

Southeast of Portsmouth on the rock-strewn shoreline of Odiorne Point, you can take in a quintessential New England seascape, with all those startling white sailboats framed by the dark-blue Atlantic. Along the shore you can see the Wentworth by the Sea Hotel in New Castle, and the picturesque 1872 granite Whaleback Lighthouse, on the Kittery, Maine, side of the harbor. Elsewhere in the 330-acre expanse of this state park, discover hiking trails and remnants of old World War II bunkers. For those with kids, don't miss the top-notch kid-centric science center, complete with a dangling humpback whale skeleton. *603-436-7406; nhstateparks.org*

Whaleback Lighthouse viewed from Odiorne State Park

WALPOLE

A stone's throw from the Connecticut River, Walpole is ready for its movie close-up. Filmmaker Ken Burns calls this town home, and even helped launch the Restaurant at Burdick's, a first-class French-style dining destination. Nearby, Stuart & John's Sugar House sits below Route 12 in Westmoreland, with panoramic views of the river. You can find artisanal cheese at Boggy Meadow Farm and heirloom fruit on the heights at scenic Alyson's Orchard, where chili cook-offs, apple pie fests, and pulled pork competitions enliven the peaceful atmosphere. Movie magic indeed. *walpolenh.us*

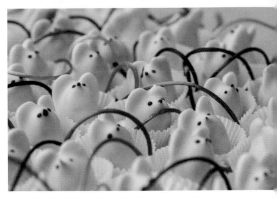

L.A. Burdick Handmade Chocolates in Walpole is an elegant café and pastry shop. Don't leave town without sampling their famous Chocolate Mice!

➡ MAPLE MANIA DESTINATIONS

One of New England's true regional treasures, maple syrup is as complex and subtly variable as fine wine. Sugarhouse tours and pancake breakfasts are ample enticements for most fans, but if you're an obsessed maple lover, you should add these ultimate experiences to your "sap bucket" list.

In Holderness, New Hampshire, you can stop at **Manor on Golden Pond** (*603-968-3348; manorongoldenpond.com*), a country B&B overlooking Squam Lake that prides itself on serving only real Homestead Maple syrup (from Chazy, NY) in its dining room. When the inn's spa added a "Maple Moments" treatment to its year-round offerings, the same supplier was tapped to provide the key ingredient. The mixture of botanical mud infused with the beloved pancake topping is said to detoxify the skin, and the comforting aroma lingers long after you shower it away.

You can enjoy maple in a different way at **Gelato Fiasco** (*207-607-4002; gelatofiasco.com*) in Brunswick and Portland, Maine. Since this gelato paradise debuted in 2007, it has masterminded more than 1,500 flavors. Sugaring-season favorite "Maple Sap Tap" is a riff on classic maple-walnut inspired by one of the founders' childhood memories of Maine Maple Sunday. Be sure to get there early, because it is made in small batches, using syrup from Skowhegan's Strawberry Hill Farms and homemade toffee.

During Vermont Maple Open House Weekend each spring in Woodstock, take the **Maple Adventure Ride** (*802-291-2419; vermontoverland.com/vomar*). You'll join 300 cyclists for this 25-mile course, which leads to a different sugarhouse each year. The maple snacks awaiting participants keep everyone pedaling.

And on Sunday afternoons in Canton, Connecticut at **Hickory Ledges Farm** (*860-693-4039; hickoryledges.com*), you can grab a stool by the woodstove in the tasting room and enjoy complimentary samples of smooth, not-too-sweet "Full Moonshine/Pete's Maple 80." This 80-proof corn liquor laced with local maple syrup is so delicious that you'll want to take home a mason jar for yourself.

SPOTLIGHT ON
LAKE WINNIPESAUKEE

As the largest lake in the state and the third largest in New England, Lake Winnipesaukee is instantly recognizable on a New Hampshire map: 71 square miles of vacation fun (more than twice the land area of Manhattan), dotted with 260 islands. The circumference is punctuated by villages, cottages, and some very fancy retreats, and the water itself is crisscrossed by every flotation device, from paddleboards to the venerable M/S *Mount Washington*, a majestic 230-foot-long excursion ship.

At the southeast corner of Winni is **Wolfeboro**, considered to be America's first summer resort. Since 1812 its heart has been the Wolfeboro Inn, with its snug rooms and the pleasant Wolfe's Tavern, where regular customers' pewter mugs hang from the ceiling. When hunger calls, it's a cinch to find everything from gourmet coffee (Seven Suns) to ice cream (Bailey's Bubble, for starters). At Mise en Place, discover the French-infused American fare that tempted former French president Nicolas Sarkozy; at Full Belli Deli, try the super-big subs that filled up Jimmy Fallon. If you like shopping, stop in at the Artisans Corner for high-quality local crafts and fine art. Outdoor enthusiasts will enjoy the Russell C. Chase Bridge Falls Path, an easy half-mile walking trail that starts beside the railroad station and leads to Wolfeboro Falls.

In **Moultonborough**, farther up Winni's eastern side, you'll find the Old Country Store and Museum: Listed on the National Register of Historic Places, it's worth visiting to pick up a memento and walk on floors seasoned with age. Nearby is the Olde Orchard Inn, a lovely place to relax, enjoy a bountiful breakfast, and amble through the property's two orchards. Moving west from Moultonborough brings you to **Center Harbor**, where you can check out Keepsake Quilting, reputed to be America's largest quilt shop; its neighboring shop, Patternworks, caters to knitting

Paddleboat cruising on the lake

fans. The bar-restaurant Canoe will meet your lunch needs and make dinner memorable with dishes such as lobster macaroni and cheese and Cajun-rubbed grilled rib-eye. After a hearty meal, you may want to take on Red Hill: The 1.7-mile hike will reward you with majestic views of Winnipesaukee and Squam Lake.

Aerial view of the lake

Ice fishing near Meredith

On the western shoreline, **Meredith** boasts some of the best accommodations on the lake. Check out the collection of four inns and two cottages that's part of the Mill Falls at the Lake complex—our favorite is elegant-rustic Church Landing, located in the former St. Charles Church and offering 70 rooms with lake views and fireplaces, two indoor/outdoor pools, a full-service spa, and fine food on-site. Topping the local dining destinations is Camp, with its fieldstone fireplace and peeled-wood trim, which serves up comfort-food classics such as mac 'n' cheese, pot roast, and even s'mores for dessert. But for breakfast, the best place is Sunshine and Pa's. About two miles out of town is Moulton Farm, a New Hampshire Agriculture Farm of Distinction, with everything from ice cream and baked goods to flowers and fresh produce. Back in town, the Mill Falls Marketplace, a converted mill, houses a variety of shops, such as Oglethorpe Fine Arts & Crafts and Vintage Diversions, chockablock with one-of-a-kind artisans' items.

South of Meredith lies **Laconia**, the home of the famous motorcycle rally held each June. Its village of Weirs Beach is a center of family entertainment, with attractions such as Logs of Fun (go-carts, climbing walls, miniature golf) and Funspot (indoor golf, bowling, bingo, arcade games galore). You can also board the huge M/S *Mount Washington* for a lake cruise. The Traveling Texas Smoke Shop provides a welcome barbecue fix, and Kellerhaus has been serving delicious ice cream and candy since 1906. Want a special treat? Try the ice-cream sundae buffet there.

In sum, there are many layers to Lake Winnipesaukee and its towns. You can walk along the water and be nearly alone, save for the company of a pair of loons, or you can play miniature golf with legions of screaming kids. You can indulge in innovative cuisine on a candlelit deck where the only noise is the whispering wind, or you can kick back with a beer and cheeseburger as the raucous pub crowd roars like a 747 on takeoff. The great thing is that everyone who comes to Winni can find his or her place. *lakesregion.org*

SPOTLIGHT ON

TOP 15 NEW HAMPSHIRE EVENTS

JANUARY

Snow Sculpting Invitational

Talented snow sculptors from across the region converge on the village of Jackson for a weekend of creating chilly masterpieces from 8-foot-high cylinders of packed snow. Although most pieces are not finished until Sunday, spectators are welcome throughout the process; nighttime illumination makes an after-dark stroll a must. In addition to the artistic endeavors, there's a bonfire for roasting marshmallows, a torchlight parade, a scavenger hunt, and plenty more to keep you entertained. *603-383-9356; jacksonnh.com*

FEBRUARY

Dartmouth Winter Carnival

Join in a weekend of seasonal fun at the oldest collegiate winter festival, held annually on campus in Hanover. Since 1910, the carnival has focused on celebrating winter, snow, and outdoor sports. Events include ski competitions, a human dogsled race, jazz and a cappella concerts, a polar bear swim, dances, and a screening of the 1939 movie *Winter Carnival*, a romance set at Dartmouth. Don't miss the huge snow sculpture the students build each year on the college green. *603-646-3399; dartmouth.edu*

Chocolate Festival

Set in Intervale and known as the "sweetest day on the trails," this is your chance to enjoy the spectacular scenery of the region as you cross-country ski, snowshoe, or drive from inn to inn, knowing that warm hospitality and divine chocolate treats await you at each stop. Your day of delightful indulgence begins by securing a festival pass at any of the participating chocolate stops along the Mount Washington Valley Ski Touring & Snowshoe Foundation network trails. *603-356-9920; mwvskitouring.org*

MARCH

Maple Weekend

For a behind-the-scenes look at how one of New Hampshire's sweetest exports is made, stop by any of the 60-plus participating sugarhouses across the state during this annual open house. Most offer tours and free samples; others also serve pancake breakfasts and let visitors take horse-drawn rides. Check the website for times and locations. *603-225-3757; nhmapleproducers.com*

APRIL

Five Colleges Book Sale

In the Upper Connecticut River Valley, book lovers have long circled one particular April weekend on their calendars: the Five Colleges Book Sale, a fundraiser that began in 1962 to support scholarships for Vermont and New Hampshire students attending Mount Holyoke, Simmons, Smith, Vassar, and Wellesley. At Lebanon High School, tables holding some 75,000 books, DVDs, CDs, books on tape, and videos are piled high and picked clean at one of New England's largest used-book sales. *five-collegesbooksale.org*

Dartmouth Winter Carnival

JUNE

Chowder Festival

For more than three decades, the oldest and largest chowder festival in New England has drawn chefs from across the Northeast to beautiful waterfront Prescott Park in Portsmouth. Bring your appetite because more than 500 gallons of clam, fish, and corn chowder will be served. Try them all! *603-436-2848; prescottpark.org*

Hampton Beach Master Sand Sculpting Competition

In case you're thinking that this is just a bunch of dabblers playing with plastic buckets and little shovels, let us assure you that it's way beyond Sandcastles 101. Artists are by invitation only, and spectators get to see what 250 tons of imported sand looks like. The scale, detail, and intricacy of these massive sculptures will surprise you, even if you're a sand-sculpture veteran. *603-926-8717; hamptonbeach.org*

JULY

American Independence Festival

A mere 26 copies from the original printing of the Declaration of Independence exist today, and one of the finest can be viewed at the American Independence Museum in Exeter, the host of this festive occasion. Watch a reenactment of the horseback delivery of the Declaration and a public reading, including some unconvinced hecklers. Then step lively to the beat of fife and drum while enjoying an arts and crafts sale, kids' activities, fireworks, fine food, and more. *603-772-2622; independence museum.org*

TOP 15 NEW HAMPSHIRE EVENTS (CONTINUED)

AUGUST
Festival of Fireworks

One of New England's biggest fireworks displays isn't held on the Fourth, or in a big city. It happens toward the end of August at the town of Jaffrey. Bring your family to Silver Ranch Airpark in the Monadnock region for this end-of-summer blast, which also features live entertainment, great food, and kids' games. *603-532-4549; jaffreychamber.com*

League of New Hampshire Craftsmen's Fair

The hills at Newbury's Mount Sunapee Resort are the backdrop for the oldest and best artisans' festival in the country. The first Craftsmen's Fair was held in 1933, in a barn at Crawford Notch. Today's extravaganza begins on the first Saturday in August and runs for more than a week, featuring the work of 350 artisans who are at the top of their professions. Pottery and handcraft demonstrations, a sculpture garden, and strolling musicians add to the carnival atmosphere. *603-224-3375; nhcrafts.org*

SEPTEMBER
Mount Washington Valley Mud Bowl

It's muddy, it's messy, and it's terrific fun—it's the annual Mount Washington Valley Mud Bowl. Held at North Conway's Hog Coliseum, this popular event attracts mud-football teams from all over New England and packs a history that stretches back more than three decades. Don't miss the colorful and zany Tournament of Mud Parade. *603-356-5947; mtwashington valley.org*

Hopkinton State Fair

Every Labor Day weekend the Merrimack Valley rolls out the straw-strewn red carpet to host the fun-filled Hopkinton State Fair. The largest agricultural festival in the state, this classic has been delivering farm and garden exhibits, games, rides, and amusements since 1915. *603-746-4191; hsfair.org*

OCTOBER
Fall Foliage Festival

Every year since 1947, community volunteers in the small, idyllic village of Warner have pulled together to host a big-time salute to autumn all around the town center. Discover a variety of fantastic foods, live entertainment, an apple pie bake-off, carnival rides, and a farmers' market, plus fine crafts for sale. *wfff.org*

DECEMBER
Candlelight Stroll at Strawbery Banke

Step back into a simpler time as 350 years of American history, winter traditions, and holiday celebrations unfold around you at Strawbery Banke, Portsmouth's famed living-history museum and the oldest waterfront neighborhood in the state. Activities include historic house tours, horse-drawn carriage rides, live music, traditional barrel making demonstrations, 18th-century holiday hearth cooking, tinsmith demonstrations, and more. *603-433-1100; strawberybanke.org*

Christmas at Canterbury Shaker Village

Celebrate the holiday's timeless delights by taking a candlelit stroll through the village or riding in a horse-drawn wagon or sleigh. Other delights include the Shaker Sisters' play, a magic show, caroling, and the "Gingerbread Spectacular," plus hands-on craft activities for the kids. *603-783-9511; shakers.org*

American Independence Festival

VERMONT

THE GREEN MOUNTAIN STATE

The mountains of Vermont are impossibly green—so much so that its name, given by early French explorers, literally translates as "Green Mountain." Rolling fields highlight antique red barns, and when all that green bursts into flaming color in autumn, Vermont's white-clapboard villages sparkle even brighter.

Don't let the timeless scenic beauty (and preponderance of dairy cows) fool you, however. While Vermont may be one of America's most rural states, it's blessed with everything the 21st-century visitor could want. First-class ski resorts such as Stowe, Okemo, and Sugarbush offer diversions all year round; in cities and small towns alike, chefs are serving up creative, irreproachably fresh farm-to-table cuisine. There's ready access to Vermont's famed cheese, beer, and maple syrup, but also to state-of-the-art museums, artisans' galleries, independent-shopping hubs, and outstanding bike trails.

And even though it's the only landlocked state in New England, Vermont still has its bases covered. Majestic Lake Champlain, which stretches 120 miles from north to south, more than deserves its reputation as "America's Sixth Great Lake"—and, to our mind, cements Vermont's status as a truly great getaway.

VERMONT ESSENTIALS

NORTH

BURLINGTON GREENWAY, BURLINGTON

With lakeside vistas, ice cream shops, sculptures, and swimming spots, this bike path is a cyclist's paradise. Ramble past cafés and shops, cross the bustling ferry landing, enjoy Burlington's 6 waterfront parks, and at the north end take the bridge over the Winooski River, which extends the 14-mile path to the Champlain Islands. It passes over a long, thin causeway, with only a few feet between your cycle and the water on both sides—an amazing experience for kids and adults alike. Maps and information are available at the Lake Champlain Regional Chamber of Commerce on Main Street. Time your visit to catch the stunning sunset over the distant Adirondacks. *877-686-5253; 802-863-3489.*

CHURCH STREET, BURLINGTON

In warm weather, there's nothing like letting a day slide gently by while sitting at an outdoor café along the 4-block-long Church Street Pedestrian Mall. There's a touch of Quebec, a touch of Europe, and a good dose of country Vermont all along the walkway. Street performers gather in the late afternoon and entertain into the night. People walk their dogs, children scamper about, and eating and drinking at a leisurely pace becomes your way of life—even if only for a day. Stop at Leunig's Bistro, which has been around since the mall opened in the early 1980s. The feel is Old World; the menu skews French. Close your eyes, feel the sun slanting across the tops of the gaily colored umbrellas, and revel in the feeling of Paris in New England. *802-863-1648; churchstmarketplace.com*

Church Street Marketplace Pedestrian Mall

A statue of Samuel de Champlain on Isle La Motte.

DOG MOUNTAIN, ST. JOHNSBURY

The home of the world's only dog chapel is just a Frisbee toss (OK, three miles) from downtown St. Johnsbury. The petite chapel truly feels like a sacred space, complete with pews and stained glass, and its walls are filled with poignant photo tributes to bygone canine pals. Perched on a hill amid 150 rolling acres, the chapel is just one part of this property designed for humans and their pups, which also offers hiking trails, a dog agility course, and displays of Stephen Huneck's colorful dog-oriented art. *802-748-2700; dogmt.com*

ECHO LEAHY CENTER FOR LAKE CHAMPLAIN, BURLINGTON

America's "Sixth Great Lake" is the focus of this waterfront aquarium and science center, where visitors come face to face with Champlain's denizens. Frogs and whale skeletons, shipwrecks and sea monsters—there's something to stir any imagination at this remarkably well-done exploration of the ecology and culture of Lake Champlain. *877-324-6386; echovermont.org*

FAIRBANKS MUSEUM & PLANETARIUM, ST. JOHNSBURY

This very Victorian "cabinet of curiosities" is the oldest science education museum (1891) in the country. Capped by a 30-foot-high barrel-vaulted ceiling, the main hall is filled with cabinets that display thousands of animal specimens, from mice and moose to bats and birds. The planetarium, meanwhile, presents the night sky as seen from Vermont's Northeast Kingdom. *802-748-2372; fairbanksmuseum.org*

HILL FARMSTEAD BREWERY, GREENSBORO

Shaun Hill grew up knowing he wanted to do something viable with his grandfather's former dairy farm in the Northeast Kingdom, a family homestead for more than two centuries. Then a school science project on fermentation set his course. More than 20 years later, this self-taught brewer is turning out nationally acclaimed pale ales, saisons, stouts, and porters that look, and drink, like fine bottles of wine. You can't buy these treasures in stores—or even bars outside Vermont—which makes going to their source one of New England's great pilgrimages. *802-533-7450; hillfarmstead.com*

ECHO Leahy Center

Kingdom Trails

JOHNSON WOOLEN MILLS, JOHNSON

Johnson's durable woolen shirts, jackets and pants are cut and stitched using traditional methods inside a modest clapboard building along the Gihon Rive. Next door is the original mill (now the factory store), which started turning local farmers' sheep wool into fabric back in 1842. Today, Johnson Woolen Mills is led by fourth-generation owner Stacy Barrows Manosh, who says of her company's long-lived popularity, "I guess people still like old-time value . . . I do know that every sugarhouse in Vermont has a Johnson Woolen Mills shirt hanging inside it!" Walk through their doors and browse through this American classic, and maybe take a piece of history home with you. *877-635-9665; johnsonwoolenmills.com*

KINGDOM TRAILS, EAST BURKE

When it comes to the Northeast Kingdom, Vermont puts on its finest pastoral dress. Wave after wave of unspoiled hillsides form a vast sea of green while small villages and farms spread out in the distance under a few soaring summits. The best way to see this glorious realm may be the legendary 150-mile mountain biking circuit simply called the Kingdom Trails, linking former farming roads with slender single-track trails. One moment, you're biking leisurely past a barn or maple

syrup shack, the next you're zooming through the tall barren pines. In fact, it's such a magnificent ride that you'll want to keep cycling even when your CamelBak runs dry. *802-626-0737; kingdomtrails.org*

LAKE CHAMPLAIN FERRIES, BURLINGTON

Founded in 1826, this venerable ferry is just the ticket for a scenic ride across Vermont's "Great Lake." There are three crossings to choose from, covering different portions of Champlain and ranging from about 15 minutes to an hour. We recommend opting for the latter, which is a seasonal offering between Burlington and Port Kent, New York, that traverses the broadest and most majestic part of Champlain. Spectacular views of the Green Mountains and Adirondacks, along with lake vistas to the north and south, elevate this ferry ride above the rest. *802-864-9804; ferries.com*

LAKE WILLOUGHBY, EAST BURKE

Stunningly beautiful Lake Willoughby is wedged between Mounts Pisgah and Hor, each more than 2,500 feet high. A century ago this fjord-like lake, more than 300 feet deep in places, hosted competing hotels along its shores, while excursion steamboats plied the waters. Today this is a quiet, haunting place cloaked in the 7,000-acre Willoughby State Forest, deep

View of Burlington from Lake Champlain

within the Northeast Kingdom. In midsummer, the clear waters and tranquil shores of North Beach are almost empty, except for a flock of seagulls circling overhead. South Beach, nearly 5 miles down, is smaller but more popular thanks to White Caps Campground, where you can dig into camping fare for breakfast or lunch, and rent canoes or kayaks for sunny excursions.

DID YOU KNOW? Since the 17th century there have been hundreds of documented sightings of Lake Champlain's very own sea monster, nicknamed "Champ"—so keep your eyes peeled!

A cruise on Lake Champlain

White Caps Campground at Lake Willoughby

Looking out over Lake Champlain

MAD RIVER VALLEY

A bumper sticker often spotted around New England exhorts, "Mad River Glen: Ski It If You Can"—meaning, don't even think about missing out on this much-loved ski area in the Mad River Valley. But the same sentiment applies year-round to the region as a whole. Framed by the Green Mountains to the west and lush meadows that run to the Roxbury Range to the east, the Mad River Valley is Vermont's premier four-season destination. There are grand hikes to be had here, most notably on the 272-mile Long Trail: Built by the Green Mountain Club between 1910 and 1930, it's the oldest long-distance trail in the U.S. There are also lots of opportunities for cycling, horseback riding, fishing, and golfing during spring, summer, and fall, while winter brings the thrill of snow sports at Mad River Glen and neighboring Sugarbush. *800-496-3409; madrivervalley.com*

PEACHAM

When photographers search for a New England village whose images would melt the heart of any urbanite dreaming of a simpler, lovelier life, they come to this village. The handsome colonial houses of its 700 inhabitants are framed by rolling hills and the sorts of vistas and atmosphere that Hollywood looks for. You can spot

> TRAVEL TIP: Check vermontcrafts.com for a map of Artisans' Open Studio Weekend, and see Vermont artists at work.

Biking up Mt. Mansfield

Fly-fishing in Mad River Valley

View from Waitsfield, VT of the ski runs at Sugarbush

The village of Peacham

parts of Peacham in *Ethan Frome, Where the Rivers Flow North,* and especially *The Spitfire Grill,* whose director remade the general store into the title eatery. Not surprisingly, the village has attracted more than its share of artists and craftspeople. *802-748-3678; nekchamber.com*

THE SHELBURNE MUSEUM AND SHELBURNE FARMS, SHELBURNE

The longtime farming community of Shelburne, on the shores of Lake Champlain, is home to a pair of one-of-a-kind attractions. The **Shelburne Museum** (*802-985-3346; shelburnemuseum.org*) is the legacy of collector and preservationist Electra Havemeyer Webb, whose eclectic tastes are on full display in a collection that includes a carousel, more than 400 quilts, circus memorabilia, Impressionist masterpieces, scrimshaw, and the showstopping *Ticonderoga,* a restored 1906 Lake Champlain side-wheel steamboat. Less than 3 miles away sits **Shelburne Farms** (*802-985-8686; shelburnefarms.org*), one of New England's grandest estates: 1,400 panoramic acres on Lake Champlain; a five-story barn (which houses a cheese-making facility, an independent bakery, and more); landscaped grounds designed by Frederick Law Olmsted; and the 1888 mansion built by William Seward Webb and Lila Vanderbilt Webb, now a gracious inn. The nonprofit farm produces award-winning farmhouse cheddar and offers walking trails, a children's farmyard, and special events such as the Vermont Cheesemakers Festival.

SMUGGLERS' NOTCH STATE PARK, STOWE

Straddling a sharply ascending corkscrew of a road sentineled by 1,000-foot cliffs, one of Vermont's most popular parks draws hikers, campers, and those who simply want to navigate the notch by car, narrowly squeezing through towering boulders. The Long Trail crosses the road at one point, and even if you are averse to hiking, you may be tempted to stroll the ¼-mile path to spectacular Bingham Falls. The steep, mile-long Sterling Pond Trail, which begins at the crest of the notch, summits at the eponymous jewel of a pond, one of the state's highest bodies of water. *888-409-7579; vtstateparks.com*

> **TRAVEL TIP:** Passing through Shelburne? Stop at the Vermont Teddy Bear Company for a tour, and get a custom-made bear for that special person in your life.

Historic Shelburne Farms

The steamboat Ticonderoga at the Shelburne Museum

→ SKIING VERMONT

When snow falls soundlessly on the mountains of Vermont, you can still hear something in the air—the sound of excited expectation. So many mountains and trails to explore, so little time. Some ski resorts begin pumping snow as early as October's first frosts, and diehards do not stop until May.

If you love local mountains with a vintage atmosphere, there's **Magic Mountain** (*802-804-5645; magicmtn.com*) in Londonderry, which recalls the early

days of the sport's popularity. These steep, narrow, twisting trails define classic New England skiing, but Magic isn't all tough terrain. While it has its share of double black diamonds, it's also popular with novice and intermediate cruisers, who flock to the mountain's southerly flank.

Skiers on a budget head to Middlebury College's **Snow Bowl** (*804-443-7669; middle burysnowbowl.com*), where a full day pass will be roughly half the price of a mega-resort. The area has been open to the public since its first trails were cut by students and Civilian Conservation Corps workers in the 1930s. The grooming is first-rate, giving the slopes a clean-cut, Ivy League corduroy look, and the terrain is remarkably varied for a small area. From the summit, views open to the peaks of the central Green Mountains rising to the north, south, and east. And if you work up an appetite, the chow in the big sunny lodge is just about the most reasonably-priced in the state.

Smugglers' Notch Resort (*800-419-4615; smuggs.com*) in Jeffersonville is always rated among the top ski destinations for families in the country, while the ski purist will find **Mad River Glen** (*800-496-3409; madriver valley.com*) a defiant throwback, with its deliberate paucity of grooming and snowmaking, exclusion of snowboards, and legendary single chairlift. But what truly makes Vermont the hub of New England skiing is its collection of major mountains— **Burke, Jay Peak, Stowe, Killington, Sugarbush, Mount Snow,** and **Okemo**— where vertical rise, trail variety, snowmaking, and grooming create a winter wonderland like no other in the East. *802-223-2439; skivermont.com*

CENTRAL

BILLINGS FARM & MUSEUM, WOODSTOCK

Established by the railroad magnate when he returned to his native Woodstock in 1871, Frederick Billings's model farm still showcases champion Jersey cows, Southdown sheep, and magnificent draft horses. Visit the 1890 farm manager's home and creamery; learn about farm work of yesteryear and today; and climb aboard for horse-drawn wagon and sleigh rides. Interactive farm programs change with the seasons. *802-457-2355; billingsfarm.org*

Scenes from Billings Farm & Museum in Woodstock

COLD HOLLOW CIDER MILL, WATERBURY

Though cider is pressed here year-round, the real reason to visit is the cider doughnuts. The recipe is a secret mix of fresh cider, whole wheat, cinnamon, and cloves. The eccentric machine runs nearly round-the-clock, dropping rings of dough into vegetable shortening, frying them for a minute, and transferring them to a conveyor belt, which lifts the cakes out of the fat and onto trays. The result is a crisp shell, a soft, slightly dry inside, and a tangy aftertaste. *800-327-7537; coldhollow.com*

KING ARTHUR FLOUR, NORWICH

Boasting the triple lure of New England, tradition, and baking, the home of America's oldest family-owned flour company runs what must be the most amply-stocked baking supply shop in New England. Not only that, but this 1790 company also offers a wide range of courses in this tastiest of the liberal arts. Some courses take only a few hours, but even if you don't have time to enroll this is a great place to stock up on necessities. You can also grab a few more exotic items, like Heidelberg Rye Sour, nonstick popover pans, and Belgian waffle makers. Take a break at the café, which serves the flakiest of croissants, pastries, and pizzas. *800-827-6836; kingarthurflour.com*

LAKE MOREY SKATING TRAIL, FAIRLEE

Make like an Olympic skater on the longest natural ice-skating trail in the country. Protected from harsh winds by the deeply forested hillsides around it, Lake Morey's 2-mile-long track is generally frozen solid from December to April. It hosts several seasonal events, including the Lake Morey Skate-athon, Lake Morey WinterFest, and a series of Nordic skating workshops, but you can also come for a quiet day of skating with family or friends amid the panoramic views of snow-covered mountainsides. *800-423-1211; lakemoreyresort.com/activities*

MONTSHIRE MUSEUM OF SCIENCE, NORWICH

At Norwich's museum of science kids and kids-at-heart can walk on distant planets, examine a bee colony, hibernate with a bear, and explore more than 140 hands-on indoor and outdoor exhibits that open windows onto the worlds of nature, physical sciences, and technology. Outside, in the David Goudy Science Park, you'll find 100 acres of trails and exhibits that focus on wind, water, and the ecology of the Connecticut River Valley. Don't forget to pack bathing suits and towels—some of the most popular exhibits are also ones that get you the wettest. *802-649-2200; montshire.org*

Montshire Museum of Science

The café at King Arthur Flour

Lake Morey Skating Trail

MORSE FARM MAPLE SUGARWORKS, MONTPELIER

Maple sugaring, as Burr Morse will tell you, doesn't require fancy stainless-steel boilers and gravity-fed tubing. Simple fire-pits and recycled milk jugs work just fine, too. He should know: His family claims sugaring roots stretching back nearly two centuries, and today he sugars from the same trees his granddad once tapped. The delicious results are showcased in many ways at this farm—which includes a country store and farm-life museum—but for our money the can't-miss offering is the Morse maple creemee (soft-serve ice cream), made with a full gallon of syrup per container of creemee mix. Heavenly. *800-242-2740; morsefarm.com*

DID YOU KNOW? Sometimes it's what you don't see—billboards were banned by the state of Vermont in 1968.

Scenes from Morse Farm Maple Sugarworks

→ DRIVING ROUTE 100

Route 100 is a restless road. As it salamanders its way through the mountainous middle of Vermont, it seems perpetually on the verge of decision, only to change its mind in a mile. One minute, it's slaloming along a rocky riverbed through dense cover of birch and maple; the next, it's soaring up to a sudden vista as though God has suddenly pulled away a curtain.

Winding some 200 miles from Massachusetts to Lake Memphremagog in Vermont, this stretch of highway has been called the most scenic in New England. In some circles, it's also known as the "Skiers' Highway," since it connects Vermont's giants—Snow, Okemo, Killington, Sugarbush, Stowe, Jay—like knots on a whip.

But the road really comes into its own in autumn, hitting the peak of fall foliage not once but many times as it traces an up-and-down course along the unspoiled edge of Green Mountain National Forest. When civilization does break through, it's in the form of quintessential Vermont villages that invite travelers to stop and look around.

Leaf peeping, after all, is about more than just leaves. It's about the foliage experience—farm stands and country stores, craft galleries and hot cider. And Route 100, with its many off-the-beaten-path side trips, offers all of that in one long, winding package. Because the road never makes up its mind, you don't have to, either.

And when Route 100 finally ends, some 10 miles short of Canada, your most difficult decision is the one to turn the car around and head home. The only comfort is that you get to see the whole show over again in reverse.

PRESIDENT CALVIN COOLIDGE STATE HISTORIC SITE, PLYMOUTH

Presidential birthplaces are sprinkled throughout the United States, but Vermont has preserved an entire presidential birth *town*. Tiny Plymouth Notch is where Calvin Coolidge was born, and he was visiting as vice president when word arrived of Warren G. Harding's death in 1923. Coolidge was sworn in by his father under the light of a kerosene lamp, in a house opposite his birthplace. The visitors' center exhibit uses Coolidge's own words, objects from his life, and interactive media to relate the story of how this farm boy became our 30th president. The surrounding white-clapboard village is frozen in the 1920s, and the cheese factory his father built now produces exceptional, granular-curd cheddar. *802-828-3051; historicsites.vermont.gov*

Step inside the church Calvin Coolidge attended as a boy.

➡ VERMONT CHEESE

With the highest number of cheesemakers per capita among the U.S. states, Vermont is justifiably proud of this industry's deep roots within its borders. Truly fantastic cheeses of all types are made in the Green Mountain State, with cheddar being perhaps the most New England–y of the lot. The handiwork of most cheese-producing farms and cooperatives can be found in local grocery stores and fine cheese shops. Or, for the freshest taste, trek north and visit their operations in person.

For true one-stop shopping, make plans to attend the **Vermont Cheesemakers Festival** (*866-261-8595; vtcheesefest.com*), held each year in July or August in Shelburne. The coach barn at historic Shelburne Farms provides the backdrop for the best and most innovative examples of the cheesemaker's craft, courtesy of more than 40 award-winning Vermont producers. The one-day event offers cheesemaking and cooking demonstrations and workshops, and lots of goodies to sample—from every kind of cheese imaginable to Vermont-made specialty foods, beer, wine, and spirits. Go online to get your tickets in advance, as this foodie extravaganza can be counted on to sell out.

Can't make it to the festival? Its gorgeous venue, **Shelburne Farms** (*802-985-8686; shelburnefarms.org*), is still worth the trip. Hugging Lake Champlain, this operation is a working grower, as well as a dairy, inn, restaurant, and education center. We love everything these folks do, but their selection of cheddars—which have garnered multiple honors from the prestigious American Cheese Society several

years running—is the thing that has us really hooked.

One of the best-known Vermont cheese producers is **Cabot Creamery** (*888-792-2268; cabotcheese.coop*). This nearly 100-year-old co-op in Cabot buys milk from more than 1,200 dairy farms all over New England and upstate New York, which it then turns into everything from grocery-store staples to award-winning aged varieties and cave-ripened cloth-bound cheddars.

Sponsored by the Windham Foundation, a nonprofit dedicated to promoting rural Vermont living, the cheesemakers of Grafton have been crafting gorgeous, creamy, nutty-tasting cheddars for decades at **Grafton Village Cheese** (*800-472-3866; graftonvillagecheese.com*). Taste some for yourself at their bucolic in-town location or in Brattleboro.

Last but not least, for a truly historic perspective, head to Mount Holly and stop in at **Crowley Cheese** (*800-683-2606; crowleycheese-vermont.com*). This dairy has been making cheese by hand, in small batches, since 1824. Theirs is the cheddar that gets sliced and served with our Thanksgiving apple pie, and the block that gets grated for Aunt Roxie's mac-and-cheese. Check the website to see when folks there are cheddaring—they love visitors.

QUECHEE GORGE, QUECHEE

On Route 4, less than 8 miles east of the bucolic town of Woodstock, you arrive at what people like to call "Vermont's Little Grand Canyon." Well, okay—Vermont's version would be very little indeed if put next to Arizona's. But that's the point: When you go searching for beauty, it's best to take it as it comes, and Quechee Gorge is a small wonder. Its beautiful walls were carved thousands of years ago by retreating glaciers, and by the Ottauquechee River, which flows 170 feet below. There are walking and hiking trails along the mile-long chasm, but lazing over a picnic lunch and enjoying the stellar view might be more your speed. *802-295-6852; hartfordvtchamber.com*

> **TRAVEL TIP:** Take a big bite of Vermont without even nibbling at your wallet: Free admission is offered to all Vermont state parks and historic sites, for one June weekend every year. *800-837-6668; vermontdays.com*

ROCK OF AGES, BARRE

In the 1920s, when the first curious road-trippers began poking around, most quarrying operations posted "Keep Out" signs. Rock of Ages took the opposite approach, building a visitor center and launching a tour program. As many as 60,000 guests a year still line up to tour the world's largest deep-hole dimension granite quarry, where derricks hoist blocks that weigh as much as half a million pints of Ben & Jerry's ice cream. You can stop by for self-guided tours of the factory, where artisans use both age-old and modern tools to sculpt memorials and statuary. You're encouraged to snag a free sample of this sturdy, fine-grained stone. Don't worry: It's estimated there'll be plenty to quarry for the next 4,500 years. *802-476-3119; rockofages.com*

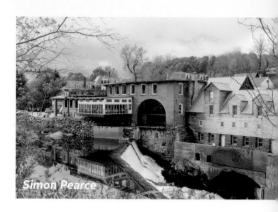
Simon Pearce

SIMON PEARCE AT THE MILL, QUECHEE

Pull open the heavy antique doors of this 19th-century woolen mill and be instantly transported into a world of beauty. Ireland-born designer Simon Pearce's coveted creations are artfully displayed for purchase within his flagship store, but that's not all. You can enjoy cocktails at the bar, served in Pearce's signature glassware beneath playful blown-glass bubble lamps, or watch as his iconic pieces are individually handmade by glass artisans in the basement workshop. Then, share farm-to-table comfort food and Pearce's private label wines in the brick-and-glass-walled restaurant overlooking a waterfall and Quechee's covered bridge. You'll want to take the exquisite tableware home. And you can. *800-774-5277; simonpearce.com*

WATERBURY FLEA MARKET, WATERBURY

Over the past 50 years, Vermont's largest and longest-running flea-for-all has grown to comprise 10 acres of antique and used furniture, household utensils, books, records, glassware, and jewelry. You'll find everything from a vintage eggbeater to a brand new canoe paddle to whole apple pies. Meanwhile, count on low vendor fees to keep the selection both reasonable and eclectic. The market is open weekends from early-May to late-October. *802-882-1919; waterburyfleamarket.com*

Queechee Gorge

Hildene in Manchester

SOUTH

The school house attended by American folk artist, Grandma Moses.

AMERICAN MUSEUM OF FLY-FISHING, MANCHESTER

For anglers, the Battenkill River is a bucket list destination. Beloved by fisherman and canoeists, the river runs south from Manchester through Sunderland and Arlington, and has been the subject of more than a few trout-obsessed writers. It's also here in Manchester that native Charles Orvis perfected the ventilated reel and opened his first store in 1856. The rest is fly-fishing history. At this charming museum, see rods and reels built by famous makers and owned by such iconic Americans as Bing Crosby, Ernest Hemingway, and Presidents Hoover and Eisenhower. *802-362-3300; amff.org*

BENNINGTON MUSEUM, BENNINGTON

This first-rate museum of art, history, and innovation is one of New England's best-kept secrets. Among its beautifully presented displays is a collection of Grandma Moses's paintings, personal belongings, and the white schoolhouse she attended as a girl. There's also a plethora of Bennington pottery, and a room full of historic glass, including gorgeous pieces by Tiffany, Loetz, and Steuben. Changing exhibitions focus on different themes, and outdoor trails take you past blooming wildflowers in the spring. *802-447-1571; benningtonmuseum.org*

FIDDLEHEAD AT FOUR CORNERS, BENNINGTON

While the stately marble building at Bennington's downtown crossroads still looks like a bank, today it is filled with carefully selected glassware, ceramics, jewelry, paintings, and fiber works from throughout North America. Take a break from browsing to play a few free games on a vintage pinball machine, pound out a tune on the 1936 baby grand piano, or unleash the kids' imaginations with chalk and blackboards in the Graffiti Vault, once the bank's walk-in safe. *802-447-1000*

HILDENE, MANCHESTER

Abraham Lincoln's first son, Robert Todd Lincoln, had vacationed in Manchester as a boy, and came back four decades later in 1905 to build Hildene. By then he had become a wealthy lawyer and railroad executive, and this 24-room Georgian Revival summer home reflects the success he found. There are many original furnishings and Lincoln family effects, and the 412-acre grounds offer walking trails, magnificent formal gardens, and a lovely Taconic Range backdrop. Listen to Robert Todd Lincoln's splendid story, which shines light on his father's great accomplishments, and on American history. *802-362-1788; hildene.org*

Fiddlehead at Four Corners

MOUNT EQUINOX SKYLINE DRIVE, SUNDERLAND

Part of the Taconic Mountain range rather than the Green Mountains, the prominent peak of Mount Equinox is the property of a Carthusian monastery. It features a 5.2-mile hairpin toll road known as the Skyline Drive, which traverses the monks' mountain fastness, climbing to a 3,835-foot elevation that commands views of the Battenkill Valley, the Massachusetts Berkshires, and the Green Mountains. Under superlative conditions you might even spot the White Mountains in New Hampshire and the Adirondacks to the west. Up top, there's a skein of hiking trails and space for hang gliding, if that's your pleasure. *802-362-1114; equinox mountain.com*

SCOTT FARM, DUMMERSTON

Landmark Trust USA manages these 626 pristine acres in southern Vermont, where a team of orchardists tends more than 100 varieties of low-spray heirloom and unusual apples. This beautiful property served as the location for the orchard scenes in *The Cider House Rules*. There's a farm stand, plus classes on pruning and grafting, pie baking, and cider making. Great bonus: For a one-of-a-kind weekend getaway, you may rent one of the many historic structures on the farm or on the adjoining Rudyard Kipling estate, Naulakha, where he wrote his *Jungle Book* series. Write your own masterpiece in his office, walk in his garden, and play pool on his table. *802-254-6868; landmarktrustusa.org*

Scenes from Scott Farm in Dummerston

UNIVERSITY OF VERMONT MORGAN HORSE FARM, WEYBRIDGE

Vermont's state animal has a special home near Middlebury, where the strong, clean-limbed descendants of the first Morgan horse roam 200 of the greenest, prettiest acres around at this breeding and training farm. On the tour, you will walk through the slate-roofed stables and hear the story of this iconic horse, beloved by presidents and farmers alike. There's a gift shop, too, but the best part is taking in the scenery and watching the foals frolic in the pastures. *802-656-3131; uvm.edu/morgan*

VERMONT COUNTRY STORE, WESTON

Looking for a flannel nightie, a manual typewriter, old-time candies . . . all in one store? That barely begins to describe the diversity of the inventory at this Vermont institution, founded in Weston in 1946; there's also a second, newer location in Rockingham. You'll find both the expected (maple syrup, wheels of cheddar) and the unexpected (pants stretchers, anyone?) in the aisles here. Plus, nostalgia is sold by the scoop at the shop's sprawling penny-candy counter. From Mary Janes to Bit-O-Honeys to Root Beer Barrels, there are hundreds of options, all self-serve— just open a paper bag and get to work. *802-824-3184; vermontcountrystore.com*

A sampling of wares at the Vermont Country Store

(This page and opposite, top) Scenes from the University of Vermont Morgan Horse Farm

VERMONT INN-TO-INN WALKING TOUR

If you're a walker, try this idiosyncratic tour: a 4-day, self-guided ramble that averages 10 miles a day, mainly around the villages of Chester, Weston, and Ludlow. The innkeepers at the 4 participating establishments along the way will transport your bags inn-to-inn, Vermont sherpa–style, and greet you at the end of the day with a drink and a homecooked meal (possibly a featherbed or Jacuzzi, too). In the morning, you will be set on your way with a hearty breakfast, snacks for the road, a map of your walking route, and best wishes for a pleasant stroll. *vermontinntoinnwalking.com*

TRAVEL TIP: Keep track of the best places to see peak fall colors. Visit foliage-vermont .com.

WESTON PLAYHOUSE, WESTON

In 1935, a renovated church on a classic village green became the setting for the Weston Playhouse, today Vermont's oldest professional theater. Although that building was lost to fire in 1962, its stately Greek Revival replacement is home to talented equity companies that bring drama, comedy, and musicals to Weston each summer for a fraction of Broadway prices. Downstairs, the West Town Eatery offers dinner before the show, and cabaret after. Adding to the cultural cachet is the new, associated Center for the Arts at Walker Farm, which promises to turn Weston into a year-round destination for the performing arts. *802-824-8167; westonplayhouse.org*

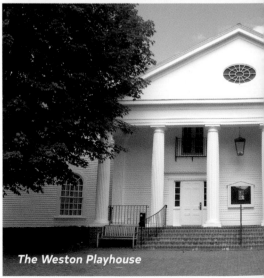

The Weston Playhouse

Road and barn (below) along the Vermont Inn-to-Inn Walking Tour

SPOTLIGHT ON

THE LAKE CHAMPLAIN ISLANDS

Summer sojourners looking to enjoy Lake Champlain often head for Vermont's **Sandbar State Park** (*802-893-2825; vtstateparks.com/sandbar*), with its broad beach and convenient location, just a few miles from Burlington. But the more curious among you might wonder just what lies at the other end of that long causeway, swinging out into the lake past the park. That can't be New York, so close. But it certainly isn't the Vermont mainland, either.

That green horizon belongs to the **Champlain Islands**, one of the big lake's greatest treasures. Twenty-eight miles long, barely 4 miles across at their widest point, the three bridge-linked main islands and one peninsula of Grand Isle County offer spectacular water's-edge views of the Green Mountains and Adirondacks. And they feature myriad ways to get out and enjoy the lake and its surrounding attractions.

From Burlington head north on Route 89 and then west on the Theodore Roosevelt Highway (Route 2). The first island on the western end of the causeway is **South Hero**, possibly named for one of

Vermont's two Revolutionary-era heroes, brothers Ethan and Ira Allen. If you come at the tail end of summer or in early fall, you will find one of the island's traditional crops at **Allenholm Farm and Hackett's Orchard** (*802-372-5566; allenholm.com*), with row upon row of trees bearing more than a dozen apple varieties. A newer kind of crop flourishes along South Hero's New York–facing side, at **Snow Farm Vineyard** (*802-372-9463; snowfarm.com*), where the islands' mild microclimate helps nurture an assortment of award-winning red and white wine grapes.

West Shore Road is a scenic alternative to Route 2 for meandering northward through the islands, and a favorite among cyclists who enjoy the Vermont countryside without its famously daunting hill climbs. Soon after the side roads divert back to the highway, a drawbridge scoots traffic across to **North Hero**, named, you guessed it, for the other Allen brother. A quick right marks the entrance to **Knight Point State Park** (*802-372-8389; vtstate parks. com/knightpoint*), the summer home of Herrmann's Royal Lipizzan Stallions. These

A quirky interior beckons visitors to Hero's Welcome General Store.

A view of Lake Champlain from Ruthcliffe Lodge

famed white horses keep the centuries-old Austrian military tradition of precision leaps and jumps alive.

The area's prettiest village clusters around North Hero's City Bay. Here, the **Hero's Welcome General Store** (*802-372-4161; heroswelcome.com*) offers everything from guidebooks to kitchenware, rents watercraft and bikes, and provides dockside picnic tables for enjoying its custom sandwiches, soups, and chili. A few doors away, the shipshape North Hero House boasts the islands' choicest accommodations and meals. If you get the chance, opt for one of the lakefront rooms with private screened deck, facing the sunrise.

Continue north past Carry Bay, where the next bridge carries the road to the **Alburg Peninsula**. It pokes down into the lake from Quebec and harbors the day-use state park Alburg Dunes, a beautifully desolate stretch of shoreline. Just beyond, a causeway leads Route 129 over to **Isle La Motte**, the most remote and least populated of the Champlain Islands. The main road loafs through table-flat farmland, but the best way to see this 2-by-5-mile green speck in the lake is via the pokey shore roads that nearly encircle it. One of them dead-ends at Vermont's most out-of-the-way accommodation and dining surprise, **Ruthcliffe Lodge** (*802-928-3200; ruthcliffe .com*), which offers snug, cheerful rooms and Italian-inspired fresh seafood dinners.

For working up an appetite, nothing beats taking out one of the inn's canoes or kayaks, watching seabirds and herons fish in the shallows. One scenic 3-mile round trip follows the coast down across Wait Bay to a tiny, rock-girt island just off Reynolds Point. According to an old story, John Philip Sousa saw a flag snapping in the breeze here and was inspired to write the instrumental arrangement for "The Star-Spangled Banner." With the great expanse of Lake Champlain spreading south past the horizon, North Hero to port, and the rugged New York shore to starboard, you don't have to be a famous composer to enjoy a sublime moment of inspiration.

The dockside picnic tables at Hero's Welcome General Store.

SPOTLIGHT ON
WOODSTOCK

Woodstock is one of many villages in New England that beg you to park your car once and return to it only when it's time to go home. But it is without rival in its variety of outdoor and indoor treats within a short walk of its center. Even better, in each season there's something to do and explore.

Take Route 4 west from I-89, just north of the junction with I-91. It will take you right downtown. Central and Elm Streets are home to bookshops, a general store, and a variety of boutiques with designer clothing, high-end home decor, and furnishings. When you're busy shopping, though, it's easy to miss the town's most unique feature: The power lines in this district are buried. It's one of many improvements funded by Laurance and Mary French Rockefeller, whose largess has helped preserve the town's historic architecture and rural heritage.

In 1968, when the town's inn needed updating, the Rockefellers stepped in. An entirely new building was built just behind the old one, which was then razed. Today, the **Woodstock Inn & Resort** (*888-338-2745; woodstockinn.com*) has a style that feels fresh and uniquely Vermont, with a roaring central fireplace (in cool-weather months) and an airy spa with its own courtyard hot tub. Newer on the scene is the family-friendly **506 On the River Inn** (*802-457-5000; ontheriver woodstock.com*), located 2 miles out of town on the banks of the Ottauquechee River and offering sleek country-industrial décor, an indoor pool and spa, and game rooms for rainy days.

How to spend a weekend in Woodstock? Let's count the ways. Rent a bike and tour the country roads with their tunnel-like archways of maples and oaks. Tee off at the